SKEIN FOR SKEIN

SKEIN FOR SKEIN

16 KNITTED PROJECTS

**Cheryl Potter with
Donna Druchunas, Celeste Pinheiro,
and JoAnne Turcotte**

CREDITS

President & CEO ▼ Tom Wierzbicki

Publisher ▼ Jane Hamada

Editorial Director ▼ Mary V. Green

Managing Editor ▼ Tina Cook

Technical Editor ▼ Ursula Reikes

Copy Editor ▼ Sheila Chapman Ryan

Design Director ▼ Stan Green

Production Manager ▼ Regina Girard

Illustrator ▼ Robin Strobel

Cover & Text Designer ▼ Shelly Garrison

Photographer ▼ Brent Kane

MISSION STATEMENT

Dedicated to providing quality products
and service to inspire creativity.

Skein for Skein: 16 Knitted Projects

© 2008 by Cheryl Potter, Donna
Druchunas, Celeste Pinheiro, and JoAnne
Turcotte

Martingale & Company
20205 144th Ave. NE
Woodinville, WA 98072-8478 USA
www.martingale-pub.com

Printed in China

13 12 11 10 09 08   8 7 6 5 4 3 2 1

**Library of Congress Cataloging-in-
Publication Data**

Library of Congress Control Number:
2008018940

ISBN: 978-1-56477-857-4

DEDICATION

To every knitter who has ever been inspired
to substitute one yarn for another—here's to
your success, and happy knitting to you!

ACKNOWLEDGMENTS

Special thanks to Mary Green for
believing in this project and going
above and beyond in every way.

CONTENTS

INTRODUCTION

The idea for *Skein for Skein* came from a discussion at a yarn show with friends who are also designers. As always, we talked about design trends and the fact that great patterns never die, they just get reinvented with new yarn. That no one had a book out about yarn substitution astounded us, because many yarn companies "create" new patterns by revamping popular ones with updated yarn. We decided to show you how fun and creative yarn substitution can be.

How often have you found the perfect pattern and discovered that the project yarn is discontinued—or maybe you found some great yarn but have no pattern? This has happened to me too often to mention. The only solution is to substitute same-weight yarn in your knitting—although I've learned that, skein for skein, the result is not always the same. In this book I have teamed up with three well-known designers with different areas of expertise to show you how to successfully substitute yarn.

Yarn substitution is exciting and adventurous but it can be scary, especially when you're trying to decide what to knit with that ball of handspun angora you've been saving. Or maybe you treasure a favorite sweater pattern but no longer have the yarn it calls for. You need to either fit the yarn to the pattern or a pattern to the yarn. Substituting yarn is not as easy as it sounds because even two yarns of the same weight can differ in fiber, texture, and gauge, which can lead to problems with stretch, drape, pattern stitch, and contrast—to name a few.

Same-weight yarns do not always knit up the same, so let this book be your guide through the maze of substituting yarns in your knitting.

These yarns are all the same weight. But do they knit to the same gauge? And is the fiber and texture right for your project?

What to do? We're here to help. *Skein for Skein* is a book about substituting same-weight yarns in your knitting, with an eye to how different fibers look when they are knit. Donna Druchunas, JoAnne Turcotte, Celeste Pinhiero, and I guide you through a variety of beginner to intermediate projects featuring four weights of yarn: fingering, DK, worsted, and bulky. We all show one design in each category for a total of 16 projects, each knit with two different same-weight yarns and swatched with a third yarn that exhibits very different results.

We seek to teach through example, and not all examples are positive! As designers, we provide tips and techniques, showing you some projects that produced the intended result, along with swatches that reveal less-than-desirable results. You will learn that just because yarns are labeled a certain weight does not mean that all same-weight yarns look the same when knit. A project knit with worsted-weight cotton will look and feel different from the same one knit with worsted-weight mohair, wool, or novelty yarn. The project's success depends upon the knitter's intent. Was the project supposed to show off a stitch pattern, loft easily, or drape well? After learning about these different factors and considering which yarns work best in each case, you may find you can customize a pattern just by substituting yarns you already have in your stash.

~Cheryl

MEET THE DESIGNERS

DONNA DRUCHUNAS

I live in the foothills of the Colorado Rocky Mountains, where I spend most of my time knitting and writing. I am the author of four knitting books, including *Kitty Knits* (Martingale & Company, 2008). My work has been featured in most major knitting publications, including *Family Circle Easy Knitting, Knitter's Magazine,* and *Interweave Knits.* In addition, I've edited several other knitting books, so you might say I know my way around a pattern.

Even so, I am not a perfectionist knitter or designer. I enjoy making things up as I go and experimenting with different types of yarns and colors to see how they work out. Although I love knitting from other designers' patterns, I almost never follow the instructions exactly because I always want to change something—the color, the fiber, perhaps even the armhole shaping. I believe that knitting should be fun and that each knitter should work in whatever way makes knitting relaxing and enjoyable.

As you can see with the yarn-substitution experiments in this book, there is a lot of leeway in the design process and that transfers over to the knitter. Even if you don't make up your own patterns from scratch, you can be a designer by changing the colors, textures, and fibers used in the garments you knit to suit your own lifestyle and fashion tastes. If winging it makes you nervous, be a perfectionist! If perfectionism makes you anxious, make things up as you go. If you are still worried about changing the yarn in a pattern, ask for help at your local yarn shop; the experts there will be able to help you find a perfect substitution for any pattern.

CELESTE PINHEIRO

My designs have appeared in *Knitter's Magazine, Creative Knitting, Interweave Knits,* and *Family Circle Easy Knitting,* and I design for yarn companies such as Classic Elite Yarns, and Cherry Tree Hill Yarn. I've also designed a few things for ready-to-wear, and I teach at conventions like those organized by the Knitting Guild of America.

When I first began designing sweaters about 12 years ago, my favorite aspect of designing was playing with color and texture on a basic sweater outline—the fun was in the "coloring." Now I'm still inspired by color, but I'm also intrigued by the shape of a garment and the challenge of creating a design that looks great on everybody (not just on a size 2).

When substituting yarns, you need to have a good understanding of the qualities of various fibers—stretchy, springy, or dense—and how they will look when knit. You also need the ability to look at a pattern and see whether it has the appropriate structural engineering (seams, size, or stitch) to support another fiber choice.

CHERYL POTTER

I own a hand-painted yarn company, Cherry Tree Hill Yarn, and have taught countless classes on color theory, hand-dying techniques, and designing with painted yarns. My yarns and designs have appeared in most of the major knitting magazines both in the United States and abroad, and I've created yarns and colors for other yarn companies and authored five knitting books in addition to this one.

Color has always been my focus in knitting. I'll admit, I'm not great with shape and drape, row counts and pattern stitches, but I do know how to put colors and textures together and I love how colors vary depending on the fiber used. My favorite designs are classic ones modernized with a hand-painted look. What I hope to show you in this book is how much fun it is to customize a pattern with color, texture, and fiber. Of course this will only work if the yarn is right for the pattern or vice versa.

JOANNE TURCOTTE

I live in northeastern Pennsylvania, where I spend much of my time designing at my kitchen table for Plymouth Yarn Company. There are over 100 yarns in the Plymouth line, so a big portion of my job as their design director is to produce over 400 new patterns a year.

My main design focus is on simple garments that show off a yarn's best features. This is fascinating to me because a pattern can look very different when made with a different yarn. In this book, you may very well find my designs to be the easiest to knit due to their simplicity. If you're a beginner, you may safely tackle these.

I worked for many years at a local yarn shop, and know many yarn-shop employees have the knowledge and skills to help you with yarn substitutions. There is more to it than just yard-for-yard exchange. They have the experience to evaluate a yarn's best and worst features, and are your best source for help in making suitable substitutions.

FINGERING-WEIGHT YARN

Although you can purchase thinner yarn, most knitters consider fingering weight skinny enough, and many rarely use smaller-diameter fiber. This yarn is commonly used for socks and scarves and often contains natural animal fiber such as merino, alpaca, silk, and blends. Fingering-weight yarn does not lend itself to novelty, so you rarely find it feathered, beribboned, laddered, or festooned with sequins. Although considered by some as utilitarian, more and more of this yarn gets used for open lacework as knitters eschew lace and cobweb weights for the more manageable fingering weight. Because there are many exotic blends and a myriad of colors to choose from in this versatile weight, substitution becomes that much more fun.

ROCKY MOUNTAIN STOLE

CALL OF THE WILD SHAWLETTE

VANDYKE TAM AND SCARF

LEAF LACE SHAWL

Knit in Fingering-Weight Alpaca from Frog Tree Yarns

ROCKY MOUNTAIN STOLE

By Donna Druchunas

For a luxurious but affordable stole, Donna chose a soft, smooth alpaca yarn in a light color to show off the pattern. Alpaca works especially well for lace knitting and shawls because it is less springy than wool and it drapes beautifully. This soft yarn worked up into a cuddly stole that is equally suited to wearing at the opera or while reading in bed.

If you'd like a shawl to wear over light-colored garments, a dark yarn would show off the eyelet pattern, although the individual stitches might be somewhat obscured. If you're new to knitting lace, you'll find that alpaca can be a bit more slippery to work with than wool, so you might want to use bamboo or wooden needles because they are less slick than metal or plastic and will grip your yarn.

Skill level: Intermediate ◼◼◼◻

Size: Approx 24" x 66" after blocking

MATERIALS

4 balls of Fingering-Weight Alpaca from Frog Tree Yarns (100% alpaca; 1.75 oz/50 g; 215 yds) in color 92 pale teal

Size 4 (3.5 mm) needles, or size needed to obtain gauge

Size G-6 (4 mm) crochet hook

Tapestry needle

GAUGE

One rep of full lace chart (two panels of mesh and one panel of leaves) = 6½"

SEED STITCH

(Worked over an even number of sts)

Row 1 (RS): *K1, P1, rep from * to end of row.

Row 2: *P1, K1, rep from * to end of row.

BODY

Use provisional CO on page 91 to CO 128 sts.

Work 4 rows of seed st.

Beg body lace patt: Work 4 sts in seed st as est, pm, work chart 1 on page 16 to last 4 sts, pm, work 4 sts in seed st as est.

Cont in patt until stole measures approx 54" long. End after working row 12 of chart.

Work 4 rows of seed st.

Do not BO.

BORDER

The border is worked on a garter st background. Sl the first st of each RS row as if to purl wyif. Knit the last st of every WS row tog with the next live st on the body of the stole.

With RS facing you, CO 15 sts. Starting with row 2 of chart 2, work rows 2–16 of chart once, then work rows 1–16 another 15 times. On last rep, BO all sts for row 16, working the last st of the border tog with the last st of the body.

Remove provisional CO and put sts onto needle. Rep border on other end of stole.

Weave in ends.

Soak item in tepid water until it is thoroughly wet. Place item on a flat surface or blocking board and stretch to dimensions. Secure in place with blocking wires and/ or rustproof pins, making sure to accentuate the points on the borders. Allow to dry thoroughly.

Chart 1
Body lace pattern

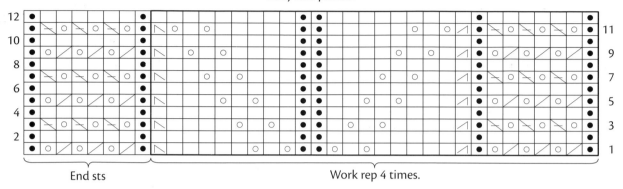

End sts

Work rep 4 times.

Chart 2
Border pattern

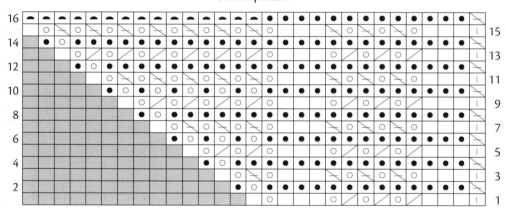

Key

☐	K on RS, P on WS	�િ K3tog	
●	P on RS, K on WS	☒ K3tog tbl	
◯	YO	⎸ sl1 wyib	
◺	K2tog	⌢ bind off	
◿	K2tog tbl (on border patt, K last st tog with next live st on body of stole)	▨ no stitch	

ALTERNATE **PICKS** AND **PANS**

While not as soft nor quite as luxurious as the alpaca stole, this Shetland wool version is easier to knit because wool yarn has a bit more "stick" on the needles. You'll find that Shetland wool is a good choice for lace knitting because it's both airy and drapes beautifully when blocked. It also holds its shape well when worn.

> A GOOD CHOICE

Yarn: 11 balls of Shetland Jumper-Weight Wool from Jamison and Smith (100% wool; 25 g; 130 yds) in color 91 bright gold

Needles: Size 4 (3.5 mm) needles, or size needed to obtain gauge

Knit in La Gran Mohair
from Classic Elite Yarns

> A NOT-SO-GOOD CHOICE

Because Donna has knit simple lace patterns and scarves with mohair before, she wanted to try it for this design, but the pattern of the lace stitches didn't show up as much as she would have liked, even after blocking.

Although she chose a light color for this swatch, the fuzzy texture of the mohair overpowered this combination of lace stitches.

When it comes to lace knitting, swatching is critical to determine if the stitch pattern is obscured by the color or texture of the yarn. Don't skip the step of blocking your swatch, because it's only when the knitting is blocked to size that the true texture and drape of the fabric can be determined.

Knit in Shetland Jumper-Weight Wool
from Jamieson and Smith

Knit in Bearfoot from Mountain Colors

CALL OF THE WILD SHAWLETTE

By Celeste Pinheiro

For this shawl, Celeste chose a hand-painted wool/mohair blend sock yarn. She liked that it had just enough mohair to lend a little fluff without being too fuzzy to blur the lace motif. The simple yarn shows the stitch pattern well, emphasizing both the airy lace and texture of the garment. Although the color may be dark for some tastes, the values of the color combinations are even with no obvious lights or darks that stand out. She loves the blend of colors in the Mountain Colors Red Tail Hawk colorway because Red Tail hawks fly over her home every day.

Celeste used size 4 needles, which may be considered large for lace work, to let the lace open up when it was blocked. Because of the darker color, the smooth yarn has sharp shadows. If this garment were knit in a lighter color, you could get away with a little more mohair content, or fuzzier yarn.

This kind of smooth, high-twist yarn is best for lace because it shows stitches clearly and blocks evenly. Also, because the yarn is mostly wool, it has both spring and memory. Because the yarn is so forgiving, areas of uneven knitting can be fixed with blocking.

Skill level: Intermediate ■■■□

Sizes: Women's S (M, L)

Top circumference: Approx 36 (40½, 45)"

Bottom circumference: Approx 48 (54, 60)"

Length: Approx 6"

MATERIALS

1 (1, 2) skein of Bearfoot from Mountain Colors (60% superwash wool, 25% mohair, 15% nylon; 350 yds) in colorway Red Tail Hawk

Size 2 (2.75 mm) needles

Size 4 (3.5 mm) needles, or size needed to obtain gauge

Tapestry needle

1 button, ¾" diameter (optional)

GAUGE

20 sts = 4" in garter st using larger needles

SHAWL

Lace patt is a multiple of 35 sts + 1 st before decs, with 8 (9, 10) reps of patt.

With larger needles, CO 281 (316, 351).

Change to smaller needles, knit 1 row.

Change to larger needles, work chart as follows:

Works rows 1–46 of chart, working rep 8 (9, 10) times.

Row 47: P2tog, *K3tog, K3, YO, K1, YO, K3, P2, K3, YO, K1, YO, K3, sl 1 kw-K2tog-psso, P3tog, rep from * to last 2 sts. Work last 2 sts in last rep as P2tog instead of P3tog—185 (208, 231) sts.

Rows 48–51: Change to smaller needles, knit.

Row 52: K0 (1, 0), *K2tog, YO; rep from * to last st, K1.

Rows 53–55: Knit.

Change to larger needle, BO all sts kw.

FINISHING

For front ties as shown in photo on opposite page, cut 3 strands of yarn about 36" long, attach to eyelet at top on one side, and braid the 3 strands. Knot ends to secure. Rep for other side.

Or for tie shown in photo on page 21, cut 3 strands of yarn about 60 (66, 72)" long. Holding three strands tog, knot one end, braid the three strands, and knot other end. Weave tie through eyelet row at top, adjust comfortably around shoulders and tie.

Or add a button at the neck and use one of the eyelets on opposite side as a buttonhole.

Weave in ends. Block lightly with a steam iron.

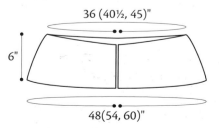

36 (40½, 45)"

6"

48(54, 60)"

Lace chart

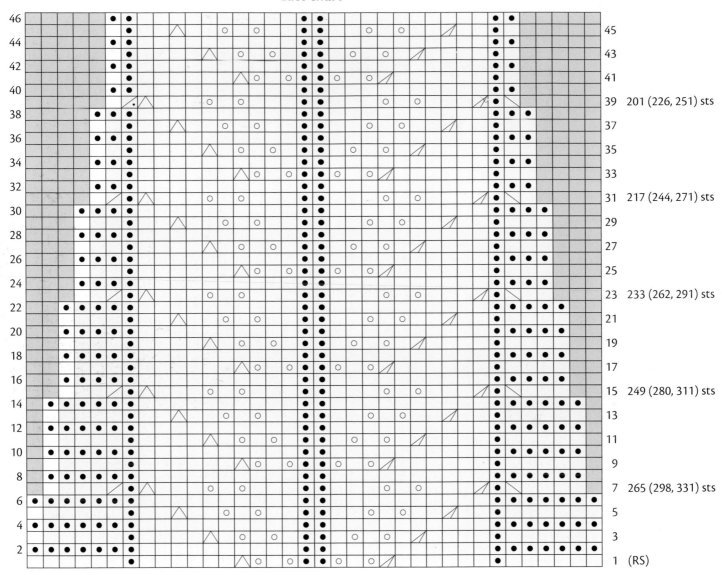

201 (226, 251) sts

217 (244, 271) sts

233 (262, 291) sts

249 (280, 311) sts

265 (298, 331) sts

Key

☐	K on RS, P on WS	◢	P2tog
●	P on RS, K on WS	◥	ssk
○	YO	▲	sl 1 kw-K2tog-psso
◿	K2tog	▧	no stitch
◿	K3tog		

ALTERNATE **PICKS** AND **PANS**

Here, Celeste chose a pima cotton/silk
blend that was both different in season
and structure yet had a similar suggested needle size. The yarn
is summery and the cotton makes it less elastic than the original wool/mohair Bearfoot blend. The wool/mohair blend is also
more airy. Because this project is a shawl, the exact gauge is
not crucial, so a slightly thinner or thicker yarn can be used
without disaster. However, substituting this yarn in a garment
where gauge is important could result in a different-sized
garment. Even with the correct gauge, knitters will finish with a
slightly firmer fabric than the mohair. Some of that firmness can
be blocked out if desired, since lace is meant to be opened up
to display the pattern.

A GOOD CHOICE

Yarn: 2 (2, 3) skeins of Lyndon Hill from Bristol Yarn Gallery
(85% pima cotton, 15% silk; 50 g; 218 yds) in color 9210 Pink

Needles: Size 2 (2.75 mm) needles and size 4 (3.5 mm) needles

Knit in Lyndon Hill from Bristol Yarn Gallery

Knit in Sassy Stripes
from Cascade Yarns

A NOT-SO-GOOD CHOICE

Here, Celeste chose a yarn
that was similar in fiber
content and suggested gauge
to her original garment—
but the color combination
has a high contrast between
lights and darks. Because the
color values have such high
contrast, the lace pattern does not show up well, and fights
with the contrast. Your eye can't decide which to focus on, so
it just doesn't want to look anymore—not a good result for a
project you spent so much time on. The knitting may be
technically beautiful, but if the color and pattern makes you
dizzy, you won't wear it (and people will avert their eyes).
This high-contrast yarn is best used in stockinette stitch projects,
or with a very simple texture such as garter or moss stitch.

Knit in Supersock from Cherry Tree Hill Yarn

VANDYKE TAM AND SCARF

By Cheryl Potter

The fingering-weight yarn used for this project is perfect for lace knitting because it is smooth enough to show a pattern stitch, practical because it is machine washable, and comes in coordinating colorways and solids so that color variation can be used in conjunction with a pattern stitch. The yarn has a lot of memory, meaning that the headband on the tam won't stretch out of shape.

The trick was to select a lace pattern that would be suitable for a coordinating set. Because the scarf is knit flat and the tam is knit in the round, I selected the Vandyke lace pattern; it's a simple one that runs in panels on the scarf but forms a star on the tam when knit in the round. A more complex or allover lace pattern would be too complicated on the tam due to the amount of decreasing needed to shape the top. The twisted cable, which was used on both items, eliminated the need for fringe on the scarf that would not have fared well in the washer.

Skill level: Intermediate ◼◼◼▢

Tam size: One size (women's Medium)

Scarf size: Approx 6½" x 48" after blocking

MATERIALS

Supersock from Cherry Tree Hill Yarn (100% superwash merino; 4 oz; 420 yds)

- **MC** 1 hank in colorway Potluck Brights
- **CC** 1 hank in color Cherry

Size 1 (2.25 mm) circular needle, 16" long

Size 3 (3.25 mm) circular needle, 16"-long and size 3 double-pointed needles, or size needed to obtain gauge

Stitch markers

Tapestry needle

GAUGE

20 sts = 4" in patt st on larger needles after blocking

TAM

Brim: With smaller needle and CC, CO 120 sts. Pm and join, being careful not to twist sts.

Work in twisted cable ribbing as follows:

Rnds 1 and 2: (K2, P2) around.

Rnd 3: (K2tog but don't slip st off needle. Instead, insert RH needle between these 2 sts and knit first st again, then sl both sts onto RH needle, P2) around.

Rnd 4: (K2, P2) around.

Work rnds 1–4 a total of 2 times, then rep rnd 1 once (total of 9 rnds).

Body: Change to larger needles and MC.

Next rnd: (K2, M1) around—180 sts.

Next rnd: (K30, pm) around. You will have 6 sections of 30 sts each. Use a different color marker for the beg of rnd.

Work 32 rnds of lace panel while alternating 8 rnds of MC and 8 rnds of CC.

Lace patt: Work Vandyke lace patt as follows or refer to tam chart on page 24.

Rnd 1: (K14, YO, sl 1 kw-K1-psso, K14) 6 times.

Rnd 2 and all even rnds: Knit.

Rnd 3: (K12, K2tog, YO, K1, YO, sl 1 kw-K1-psso, K13) 6 times.

Rnd 5: (K11, K2tog, YO, K3, YO, sl 1 kw-K1-psso, K12) 6 times.

Rnd 7: (K10, K2tog, YO, K5, YO, sl 1 kw-K1-psso, K11) 6 times.

Rnd 8: Knit.

Work rnds 1–8 a total of 4 times.

Work dec rnds as follows, alternating MC and CC every 8 rnds as est. Change to dpns as needed.

Rnd 1: (K2tog, K12, YO, sl 1 kw-K1-psso, K12, sl 1 kw-K1-psso) 6 times—28 sts between markers.

Rnd 2 and all even rnds: Knit.

Rnd 3: (K2tog, K9, K2tog, YO, K1, YO, sl 1 kw-K1-psso, K10, sl 1 kw-K1-psso) 6 times—26 sts between markers.

Rnd 5: (K2tog, K7, K2tog, YO, K3, YO, sl 1 kw-K1-psso, K8, sl 1 kw-K1-psso) 6 times—24 sts between markers.

Rnd 7: (K2tog, K5, K2tog, YO, K5, YO, sl 1 kw-K1-psso, K6, sl 1 kw-K1-psso) 6 times—22 sts between markers.

Rnd 9: Switch to CC. (K2tog, K8, YO, sl 1 kw-K1-psso, K8, sl 1 kw-K1-psso) 6 times—20 sts between markers.

Rnd 11: (K2tog, K5, K2tog, YO, K1, YO, sl 1 kw-K1-psso, K6, sl 1 kw-K1-psso) 6 times—18 sts between markers.

Rnd 13: (K2tog, K3, K2tog, YO, K3, YO, s1 1 kw-K1-psso, K4, sl 1 kw-K1-psso) 6 times—16 sts between markers.

Rnd 15: (K2tog, K1, K2tog, YO, K5, YO, sl 1 kw-K1-psso, K2, sl 1 kw-K1-psso) 6 times—14 sts between markers.

Rnd 17: Switch to MC. (K2tog, K4, YO, sl 1 kw-K1-psso, K4, sl 1 kw-K1-psso) 6 times—12 sts between markers.

Rnd 19: (K2tog, K1, K2tog, YO, K1, YO, sl 1 kw-K1-psso, K2, sl 1 kw-K1-psso) 6 times—10 sts between markers.

Rnd 21: (K3tog, YO, K3, YO, s1 1 kw-K1-psso, sl 1 kw-K1-psso) 6 times—8 sts between markers.

Rnd 23: (K2tog, K4, sl 1 kw-K1-psso) 6 times—6 sts between markers.

Rnd 25: Switch to CC, removing markers as you go. *K2tog, K2, sl 1 kw-K1-psso; rep from * around—24 total sts.

Rnds 27 and 29: *K2tog around—6 sts after rnd 29.

Break yarn and thread it onto tapestry needle. Run needle through 6 rem sts and gather; sew tight to secure.

SCARF

With larger needle and CC, CO 40 sts.

Work in twisted cable ribbing as follows:

Rows 1 and 2: (K2, P2) across.

Row 3: (K2tog but don't sl st off needle. Instead, insert RH needle between these 2 sts and knit first st again, then sl both onto RH needle, P2) across.

Row 4: (K2, P2) across.

Work 4-row ribbing for 1", ending after a completed row 1.

Change to MC and work 2 rows in K2, P2 ribbing.

Work Vandyke lace patt as follows or refer to scarf chart below.

Row 1 (RS): *(K9, YO, sl 1 kw-K1-psso, K9) twice.

Row 2 and all WS rows: Purl.

Row 3: *(K7, K2tog, YO, K1, YO, sl 1 kw-K1-psso, K8) twice.

Row 5: *(K6, K2tog, YO, K3, YO, sl 1 kw-K1-psso, K7) twice.

Row 7: *(K5, K2tog, YO, K5, YO, sl 1 kw-K1-psso, K6) twice.

Row 8: Purl.

Work 8-row lace patt, while alternating 8 rows of MC and 8 rows of CC, until scarf is 46" (or desired length), ending with row 8 in MC.

With MC, work 2 rows of K2, P2 ribbing.

With CC, work in twisted cable ribbing for 1".

BO loosely in patt.

FINISHING

Weave in ends.

Block to measurements with steam iron.

Tam chart

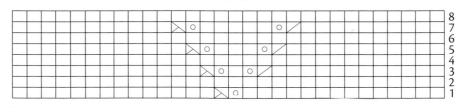

Work 30-st repeat 6 times.
All rnds of chart are worked from right to left.

Scarf chart

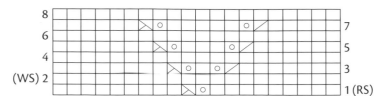

Work 20-st repeat twice.
RS rows are worked from right to left.
WS rows are worked from left to right.

Key

☐	K on RS, P on WS
○	YO
⟋	K2tog
⟋ (boxed)	sl 1 kw-K1-psso

ALTERNATE **PICKS** AND **PANS**

For this set, I used a fingering-weight alpaca that is accented by a strand of glitter in two distinct colorways, which contrast rather than coordinate. The garments are very soft and the alpaca lofted well, giving this set a warmer and more luxurious look than the first example. However, the yarn is not machine washable.

Knit in Glitter Alpaca from Cherry Tree Hill Yarn

> A GOOD CHOICE

Using two contrasting colorways makes a very lively hat and scarf set. But the combination of colorways, hairy texture, and the glitter changes the look of the projects, making them a little more over the top. The lace pattern, although visible, is a bit more difficult to discern because of the fuzzy yarn.

Yarn: 2 hanks *each* of Glitter Alpaca from Cherry Tree Hill Yarn (99% alpaca, 1% glitter; 50 g; 214 yds) in colorway Sugar Maple and colorway Wild Cherry

Needles: Size 1 (2.25 mm) 16" circular needle, size 3 (3.25 mm) 16" circular needle, and size 3 double-pointed needles, or size needed to obtain gauge

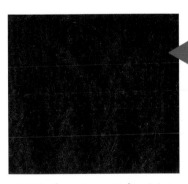

Knit in fingering-weight qiviut
from Windy Valley Muskox

> A NOT-SO-GOOD CHOICE

For this swatch, I used a solid color of an exotic and very expensive fiber. Qiviut, which comes from the down of the musk ox, is loftier and lighter than other fibers, and is very furry. Although it is fingering weight, the loft makes it knit up more like a sport-weight yarn, which can offset the price. Qivuit is incomparable in quality, and treating it as sport weight can gain you yardage in the exotic yarn arena.

Knit in Buckingham from Bristol Yarn Gallery

LEAF LACE SHAWL

By JoAnne Turcotte

Any lace pattern needs to be shown in yarn that will accentuate the openwork of the design, so for this project, JoAnne chose a firmly twisted fingering-weight yarn. Buckingham is a blend of 80% alpaca and 20% silk. The yarn's medium twist provides strong enough stitch definition to firmly hold the knit and purl stitches in place while opening up the holes created by the yarnovers in the lace pattern. A yarn with poor twist could hide or misshape the stitches and distort the overall look of the pattern design. The lack of bloom (fuzziness) also allows the yarn overs to open up the pattern's design. The light solid color shows off the lace at its best. The alpaca/silk blend blocks nicely since silk is a fiber that stabilizes the strand.

A yarn with high twist, while providing excellent stitch definition, may hold the stitches so firmly in place that maximum blocking may not be possible. Yarns with high twist tend to spring back into place, an excellent feature for some designs, but not necessarily for lacework where strong blocking is encouraged because it will accentuate the opening up of the lace.

For good blockability, check your fiber content. Natural wools, alpacas, and cottons block the best and open up the design to its fullest. If the yarn has synthetic fibers such as acrylic or nylon, the finished garment may not be highly blockable.

Skill level: Intermediate ◼◼◼▢

Size: Approx 12" x 60" after blocking

MATERIALS

3 skeins of Buckingham from Bristol Yarn Gallery (80% alpaca, 20% silk; 50 g; 218 yds) in color 9210

Size 8 (5 mm) needles, or size needed to obtain gauge

Tapestry needle

GAUGE

4 sts = 1" in patt st

SHAWL

CO 49 sts.

Knit 4 rows.

Work chart on page 28 as follows:

Row 1: K4, work first row of lace leaf chart (over center 41 sts) to last 4 sts, end K4.

Row 2: K4, work second row of lace leaf chart (over center 41 sts) to last 4 sts, end K4.

Cont working center 41 sts from chart, keeping first 4 and last 4 sts of each row in garter st, until total length is approx 59" from CO edge, or until almost out of yarn. End with row 8 or row 16.

Knit 4 rows.

BO all sts.

Block to given measurements, or as desired.

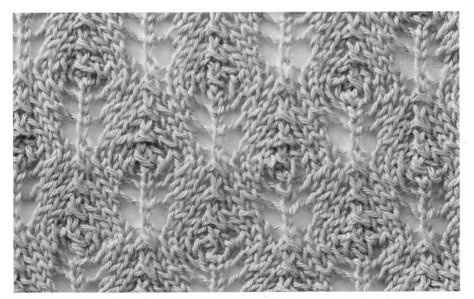

A firmly twisted yarn accentuates the open lacework.

Leaf lace chart

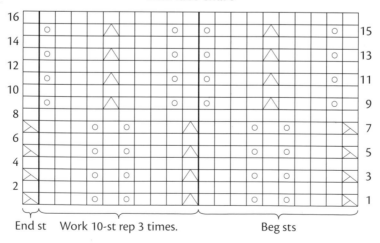

End st   Work 10-st rep 3 times.   Beg sts

Key

☐	K on RS, P on WS	⟋⟍	sl 1 kw-K1-psso
○	YO	⟋⟍	sl1 kw-K2tog-psso
⟋	K2tog		

ALTERNATE **PICKS** AND **PANS**

This luxury silk is slipperier to work with than the Buckingham alpaca/silk blend.

A GOOD CHOICE

It has a softer twist so the stitch definition is somewhat less defined than the Buckingham. The light hand-painted colorway, while adding to the overall enjoyment of the shawl, does slightly obscure the lace pattern. The beauty of the openwork shows through the color variations.

The yarn does not show any more bloom than does the Buckingham, so the yarn's texture will not blur the design. While the silk yarn does not block quite as well as the alpaca/silk blend, it does still block out enough to show off the design. However, it will require a bit more stretching and pinning to open up the pattern stitch for the shawl's final form.

Yarn: 1 hank of Cascade Fingering from Cherry Tree Hill Yarns (100% silk; 150 g; 666 yds) in color Spring Frost (a much longer scarf can be achieved, if desired, with the yardage in this yarn)

Needles: Size 8 (5 mm) needles, or size needed to obtain gauge

A NOT-SO-GOOD CHOICE

Knit in Imperiale Lace from Lane Cervinia

Lightweight luxury mohair makes a wonderful shawl, but is not the best choice for show casing an openwork design. The bloom will obscure the openwork, filling up the spaces to create a halo or blur over the entire design.

Knit in Cascade Fingering from Cherry Tree Hill Yarn

The mohair, which contains 20% nylon, does not block very well at all. Nylon holds its shape better than silk, which of course makes blocking more difficult, and limits the ability to block the lace design.

DK-WEIGHT YARN

DK-weight means "double knitting," a yarn that is somewhat lighter than worsted weight. This versatile fiber weight is often used as a transitional-season yarn, for example, winter into spring or summer into fall. Because DK yarns have the look and feel of heavier yarns without the warmth, they are popular in areas with temperate winter climates. Most recently, DK-weight yarns have gained popularity among the air-conditioned office crowd because they're thicker than sport weight and slightly thinner than worsted, but can still offer the comfortable warmth of a sweater or cardigan.

SUNSHINE LACE CARDIGAN

RUSTIC ROSES SWEATER

CABLED FRONT-PANEL SHELL

FAUX-CABLE RIBBED SOCKS

Knit in North Country Cotton from Cherry Tree Hill Yarn

SUNSHINE LACE CARDIGAN

By Celeste Pinheiro

The stitch pattern used for this lacy cardigan is one that works well with a variety of yarn choices, including cotton, because of its simplicity and large areas of stockinette stitch. The zigzag lace stripe is ideal for a decreasing yoke because the same zigzag pattern can be done in smaller stitch repeats. This cardigan is knit all in one piece, which means finishing is a breeze—there are no seams!

Because the lace pattern isn't fussy, you can use a variegated yarn without creating distraction. Choosing a smooth, firmly spun, 100%-cotton yarn gives clear stitch definition, and the result is easy to block. Because the yarn is mercerized, it won't shrink or pill.

This lace pattern is simple enough to work with a variety of yarns. You can emphasize the surface pattern in the yarn by choosing a variegated or marled yarn, or emphasize the texture by choosing a fluffy or slubby yarn.

Skill level: Intermediate ◼◼◼◻

Sizes: Women's S (M, L, XL)

Finished bust: 36 (40, 44, 48)"

Finished length to shoulder: 23½" (all sizes)

MATERIALS

4 (5, 5, 6) skeins of North Country Cotton from Cherry Tree Hill Yarn (100% combed cotton; 4 oz; 213 yds) in color Spanish Moss

Size 4 (3.5 mm) needles

Size 6 (4 mm) needles, or size needed to obtain gauge

Size G-6 (4 mm) crochet hook

Tapestry needle

6 buttons, 6½" diameter

GAUGE

17 sts = 4" in lace patt on larger needles

18 rows (1 rep of lace patt) = 2½" in lace patt on larger needles

LACE PATTERN

Multiple of 10 sts + 2 selvage sts

Row 1 (RS): With larger needles, knit.

Rows 2, 4, 6, 8, 10, 12, and 14 (WS): Purl.

Row 3: K1 (selvage), *YO, ssk, K8; rep to last st, K1 (selvage).

Row 5: K1, *K1, YO, ssk, K5, K2tog, YO; rep from * to last st, K1.

Row 7: K1, *K2, YO, ssk, K3, K2tog, YO, K1; rep from * to last st, K1.

Row 9: K1, *K3, YO, ssk, K1, K2tog, YO, K2; rep from * to last st, K1.

Row 11: K1, *K4, YO, sl 1 kw-K2tog-psso, YO, K3; rep from * to last st, K1.

Row 13: K1, *K5, YO, ssk, K3; rep from * to last st, K1.

Rows 15 and 16: Change to smaller needles, knit.

Row 17: K1, *K2tog, YO; rep from * to last st, K1.

Row 18: Knit.

Rep rows 1–18 for patt.

A simple pattern stitch shows off this variegated yarn best.

BODY

Garment is knit in one piece from hem to armhole; then armhole sts are bound off and sleeve sts added and yoke is knit in one piece. If you would like a shorter cardigan (about 21" long), omit 1 rep in body.

With larger needles, CO 152 (172, 192, 212) sts (this includes 1 selvage st at each side).

Next row (WS): Change to smaller needles, knit 3 rows.

Next row (RS): K1 (selvage), *K2tog, YO; rep from * to last st, K1 (selvage).

Next row: Change to larger needles and work 5 complete reps of lace patt (chart 1 on page 36), then work through row 15 of lace patt.

Armhole shaping (WS): P33 (38, 43, 48), BO 10 sts, P66 (76, 86, 96), BO 10 sts, purl to end.

Yoke set-up (RS): (On this row only of patt, work with larger needles, change to smaller needles on next row.) K33 (38, 43, 48), CO 50 (50, 60, 60) sts, K66 (76, 86, 96), CO 50 (50, 60, 60) sts, knit to end—232 (252, 292, 312) sts.

Cont on smaller needles, work row 18 of lace patt.

Change to larger needles and work rows 1–14 of lace patt.

YOKE

Row 15: First dec row: Change to smaller needles, K1 (selvage), *K3, K2tog; rep from * to last st, K1—186 (202, 234, 250) sts.

Work rows 16–18 of lace patt.

First lace band: Work as follows or refer to chart 2 on page 36.

Row 1 (RS): Change to larger needles, knit.

Row 2, 4, 6, 8, and 10 (WS): Purl.

Row 3: K1, *YO, ssk, K6; rep from * to last st, K1.

Row 5: K1, *K1, YO, ssk, K3, K2tog, YO; rep from * to last st, K1.

Row 7: K1, *K2, YO, ssk, K1, K2tog, YO, K1; rep from * to last st, K1.

Row 9: K1, *K3, YO, sl 1-K2tog-psso, YO, K2; rep from * to last st, K1.

Row 11: Second dec row: Change to smaller needles, K1, *K2, K2tog; rep from * to last st, K1—140 (152, 176, 188) sts.

Cont with smaller needles, work rows 16–18 of lace patt (rows 12–14 on chart 2).

Second lace band: Work as follows, or refer to chart 3 on page 36.

Row 1 (RS): Change to larger needles, knit.

Rows 2, 4, 6, and 8 (WS): Purl.

Row 3: K1, *YO, ssk, K4; rep from * to last st, K1.

Row 5: K1, *K1, YO, ssk, K1, K2tog, YO; rep from * to last st, K1.

Row 7: K1, *K2, YO, sl 1 kw-K2tog-psso, YO, K1; rep from * to last st, K1.

Row 9: Third dec row: Change to smaller needles, K1, *K1, K2tog; rep from * to last st, K1—92 (100, 116, 124).

Cont with smaller needles, work rows 16–18 of lace patt (rows 10–12 on chart 3).

BO all sts on next row.

FINISHING

With crochet hook, work sc around hem, front edges, and neck; then work rev sc (crab st) all around. Work same crochet edging around armholes. I worked 1 sc into each st, and 2 sc for every 3 rows.

Cut 6 strands of yarn, each about 120" long. Using 2 strands in 3 groups, make a braid and thread through eyelets in eyelet rows as shown in photo on page 32.

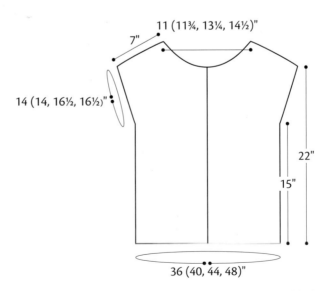

Armhole and neck circumferences adjustable (both smaller and larger) by crochet edging.

These measurements are determined by row gauge.

ALTERNATE **PICKS** AND **PANS**

For a cooler-weather garment, Celeste chose a DK-weight alpaca yarn. The

A GOOD CHOICE

heathery look of the alpaca shows the simple lace pattern almost as well as the original, even though it is a fuzzier yarn. Even with frequent wear, the firm crocheted edging will prevent the garment from sagging, and the stockinette heavy lace pattern has so few lacey holes that this cardigan is ideal for winter warmth. Working a lace design in a winter yarn is a little unexpected, but the results can be beautiful. Imagine it worn over a turtleneck, for example.

The alpaca is more elastic than cotton, and when finished, the garment drew into itself slightly. Although this was easily corrected with blocking, knowing how a fiber behaves can save you from apparent disappointment!

To finish this version, add buttons on the eyelet rows, using the opposite eyelet for the buttonhole.

Yarn: 7 (8, 9, 10, 11) skeins of Inca Alpaca from Classic Elite Yarns (100% alpaca; 50 g; 109 yds) in color 1142

Needles: Size 4 (3.5 mm) needles and size 6 (4 mm) needles, or size needed to obtain gauge

Knit in Inca Alpaca from Classic Elite Yarns

Knit in Linen Isle
from Plymouth Yarn Company

A NOT-SO-GOOD CHOICE

While this yarn has a nice look and feel and shows off the lace pattern nicely, it is a single ply, giving it a tendency to stretch on the bias. With yarns that stretch diagonally, knitters must be careful to choose an appro-priate design, such as a lace pattern with balanced "K2tog" and "ssk," or cables that twist in opposite directions, or pullovers with carefully finished invisible seams.

A yarn like this would work well for a garment that doesn't need to drape a certain way, such as a shawl, or a pullover knit in the round, where there are no open front edges to emphasize the bias effect.

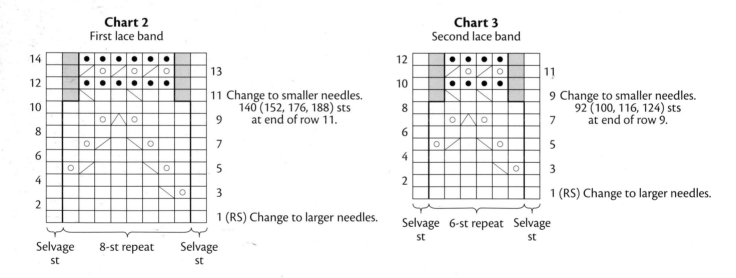

Chart 1
Body

18 ● ● ● ● ● ● ● ● ● ●
17
16 ● ● ● ● ● ● ● ● ● ●
15 Change to smaller needles.
14
13
12
11
10
9
8
7
6
5
4
3
2
1 (RS) Change to larger needles.

Selvage st — 10-st repeat — Selvage st

Key
☐ K on RS, P on WS
● P on RS, K on WS
○ YO
╱ K2tog
╲ ssk
⟋⟍ sl 1 kw-K2tog-psso
▩ no stitch

Chart 2
First lace band

14
13
12
11 Change to smaller needles.
   140 (152, 176, 188) sts
   at end of row 11.
10
9
8
7
6
5
4
3
2
1 (RS) Change to larger needles.

Selvage st — 8-st repeat — Selvage st

Chart 3
Second lace band

12
11
10
9 Change to smaller needles.
   92 (100, 116, 124) sts
   at end of row 9.
8
7
6
5
4
3
2
1 (RS) Change to larger needles.

Selvage st — 6-st repeat — Selvage st

RUSTIC ROSES SWEATER

By Cheryl Potter

Knit in Silk and Merino DK from Cherry Tree Hill Yarn

Instead of using bulky wool, I gave a traditional Icelandic pullover a more modern look by using a thinner yarn that's suitable for a variety of climates. Both a brighter palette and luxury fiber—a silk/wool blend—offer the garment a fresh look and feel. Instead of using a variety of solid-colored yarns, I opted for two hand-painted colorways, and two solids.

The sweater looks complicated, but only a few colors are used and only two colors are used in any one row. The effect looks intricate and the simplicity is wonderful. Knitters will feel as if they're cheating!

When working with hand-dyed or hand-painted yarns (ones that have variation within the color), it's important to keep the contrast high between the colorways so that the pattern won't become lost. Keep the contrast high *between* colors, not *within* colors.

Skill level: Intermediate ◀■■▯

Sizes: Women's S (M, L, XL)

Finished bust: 40 (44, 48, 52)"

Finished length: 22, (23, 24, 25)"

MATERIALS

Silk and Merino DK from Cherry Tree Hill Yarn (50% merino wool, 50% silk; 4 oz; 313 yds)

- **MC** 4 (5, 5, 6) hanks of Wild Cherry
- **A** 1 hank of Burgundy
- **B** 1 hank of Green Mountain Madness
- **C** 1 hank of Loden

Size 4 (3.5 mm) circular needles, 16" and 24" long, and size 4 double-pointed needles

Size 6 (4 mm) circular needles, 16", 24", and 32" long, and size 6 double-pointed needles, or size needed to obtain gauge

Stitch holders or spare needle

Tapestry needle

GAUGE

20 sts and 20 rows = 4" in St st on larger needle

BODY

With 24"-long size 4 circular needle and MC, CO 90 (100, 110, 120) sts, pm, CO 90 (100, 110, 120) sts, pm, join for a total of 180 (200, 220, 240) sts.

Work in corrugated ribbing for 14 rnds as follows:

Rnd 1 (set-up rnd): (K2 with MC, P2 with A) around.

Rnds 2–14: (K2 with MC, P2 with A) around.

Inc rnd: With MC, *K8 (9, 10, 11), K1f&b; rep from * around—200 (220, 240, 260) sts.

Change to 32"-long size 6 circular needle and knit 1 rnd even.

Rustic rose patt: Work 18 rnds of chart 1 on page 40, working only sts 1–20 of chart a total of 10 (11, 12, 13) times around.

With MC, cont in rnd until piece measures 13 (13½, 14, 14½)" from beg. Place sts on a holder or spare needle.

Hand-painted yarn gives the rose motif the complex look of a watercolor.

SLEEVES

With smaller dpns, CO 40 sts with MC. Pm and join into rnd. Work in corrugated ribbing for 13 rnds as follows:

Rnd 1 (set-up rnd): (K2 with MC, K2 with A) around.

Rnds 2–14: (K2 in MC, P2 with A) around.

Inc rnd: With MC, inc 5 (5, 7, 7) sts evenly around—45 (45, 47, 47) sts.

Change to larger dpns, work 1 rnd even.

Switch to 16"-long size 6 circular needle when enough sts are on needles.

Rustic rose patt: Work 18 rnds of chart 1, working 1 (1, 2, 2) sts in color of first st, work sts 1–22 of chart twice, work 0 (0, 1, 1) sts in color of last st. AT SAME TIME inc 1 st on each side of marker every fifth rnd 6 (7, 8, 9) times—57 (59, 63, 65) sts, then every sixth rnd 7 times—71 (73, 77, 79) sts. Work new sts in plain color while working chart section.

After rose patt is complete, cont in MC until sleeve measures 16 (16 ½, 17, 17½)", ending last rnd 8 sts before marker. Place next 16 sts on holder. Place rem 55 (57, 61, 63) sleeve sts on spare needle.

JOIN SLEEVES AND BODY

Work 84 (94, 104, 114) body sts, place next 16 sts for underarm on holder (remove marker), work 55 (57, 61, 63) sts of right sleeve, work 84 (94, 104, 114) body sts, place next 16 sts for underarm on holder (remove marker), work 55 (57, 61, 63) sts of left sleeve—278 (302, 330, 354) sts. Pm at beg of rnd. The 16 sleeve sts on each holder will match the 16 body sts on each holder and will be joined later.

YOKE

With 32" circular needle and MC, work even for 1 rnd.

Switch to shorter size 6 circular needle as needed.

Next rnd: Cont with MC, dec 2 (2, 0, 0) sts evenly spaced—276 (300, 330, 354) sts.

Work rows 1–5 of chart 2 on page 40.

Work 1 (2, 3, 3) rnds even in MC, dec 3 (6, 10, 14) sts evenly spaced around—273 (294, 320, 340) sts.

Rustic rose patt: Work 17 rows of chart 1, working sts *1–21 (1–21, 1–20, 1–20); rep from * around.

Dec rnd: With MC, K10 (3, 0, 6), (K2, K2tog) 30 (36, 40, 41) times, K11 (3, 0, 6), (K2, K2tog) 33 (36, 40, 41) times—210 (222, 240, 258) sts.

Work rows 1–5 of chart 2 again.

With MC, knit 1 (2, 2, 3) rows even.

Dec rnd: With A, K0 (6, 10, 3), [K3 (3, 3, 4), K2tog)] 21 (21, 18, 21) times, K0 (6, 10, 3), [K3 (3, 3, 4), K2tog)] 21 (21, 18, 21) times, K0 (0, 10, 0), (K3, K2tog) 0 (0, 6, 0) times—168 (180, 198, 216) sts.

With A, work 1 (1, 2, 3) rnds.

With C, work 2 (2, 3, 3) rnds.

Dec rnd: With C, K3 (0, 3, 0), [K7 (8, 6, 7), K2tog] 9 (9, 12, 12) times, K3 (0, 3, 0), [K7 (8, 6, 7), K2tog] 9 (9, 12, 12) times—150, (162, 174, 192) sts.

Cherry motif: Work rows 1–11 of chart 3 on page 40.

Dec rnd: With MC, (K1, K2tog) 50 (54, 58, 64) times—100 (108, 116, 128) sts.

With MC, work 1 (1, 1, 2) rows even

Dec rnd: With MC, K2 (4, 4, 0), K2tog 0 (0, 2, 4) times, [K6 (3, 3, 2), K2tog] 6 (10, 10, 14) times, K2 (4, 4, 0), K2tog 0 (0, 2, 4) times, [K6 (3, 3, 2), K2tog] 6 (10, 10, 14) times]—88 (88, 92, 92) sts. With smaller 16" needle, MC, and A, work 8 rows of corrugated ribbing as for body border on page 38. BO all sts loosely.

FINISHING

Sew underarm sts on holders tog using kitchener st.

Weave in all ends. Block gently.

Chart 1

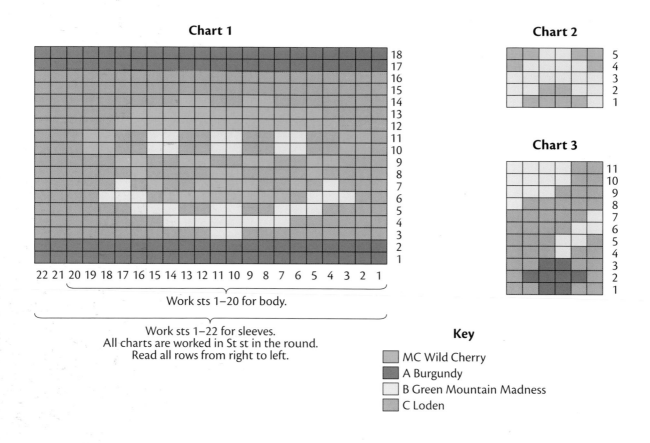

18
17
16
15
14
13
12
11
10
9
8
7
6
5
4
3
2
1

22 21 20 19 18 17 16 15 14 13 12 11 10 9 8 7 6 5 4 3 2 1

Work sts 1–20 for body.

Work sts 1–22 for sleeves.
All charts are worked in St st in the round.
Read all rows from right to left.

Chart 2

5
4
3
2
1

Chart 3

11
10
9
8
7
6
5
4
3
2
1

Key

MC Wild Cherry
A Burgundy
B Green Mountain Madness
C Loden

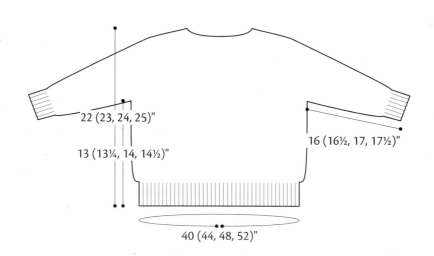

22 (23, 24, 25)"

16 (16½, 17, 17½)"

13 (13¼, 14, 14½)"

40 (44, 48, 52)"

ALTERNATE **PICKS** AND **PANS**

For this version, I used South West Trading Company's Bamboo yarn, which is one of the newer environmentally conscious fibers, and not something knitters would associate with a traditional ethnic sweater. Choosing solid colors emphasized the Fair Isle pattern, and the crispness of the fiber made it easy to work with on the needles. However, bamboo behaves more like cotton yarn than like wool, which meant it wasn't as easy to weave in the ends on the finished garment—and there are many ends to weave!

A GOOD CHOICE

The rose pattern stands out well in the solid-colored yarns, and the garment can be worn in a variety of climates—even the southwest, where the yarn originates. Because the colors don't merge into each other as in hand-painted colorways, the color changes (and any mistakes) are more obvious.

Yarn: Bamboo Yarn from South West Trading Company (100% bamboo; 100 g; 250 yds)

> **MC** 9 (10, 11, 12) balls of Navy
> **A** 2 balls of Fuchsia
> **B** 2 balls of Jade
> **C** 2 balls of Electric Blue

Needles: 2 size 4 (3.5 mm) circular needles, 16" and 24" long; 3 size 6 (4 mm) circular needles, 16", 24", and 32" long; and size 4 and size 6 double-pointed needles, or size needed to obtain gauge

Knit in Bamboo from South West Trading Company

Knit in Minnie
from Classic Elite Yarns

A NOT-SO-GOOD CHOICE

Minnie is a DK-weight variegated mohair blend yarn with novelty flecks. This yarn was not only lofty, but also very busy. Frankly, it had too much texture to discern the Fair Isle motif. The mohair and space-dyed color changes and random flecks of additional color obscured the pattern stitches. The result was a distracting area of Fair Isle in which the roses could not be distinguished as part of the pattern, one of the many pitfalls of attempting to impose a pattern upon novelty yarn.

While using hand-painted yarns with subtle color variation or a specialty fiber like bamboo both lend a modern flare to a traditional Fair Isle look in the samples above, here the novelty flecks and mohair texture along with the variegated color creates a fabric in which the pattern is no longer visible. This yarn is perfect in a project where the pattern can be random, which is a benefit to the beginner knitter.

Knit in Super Taj Mahal from Lane Cervinia

CABLED FRONT-PANEL SHELL

By JoAnne Turcotte

A soft blend of merino, silk, and cashmere is a perfect choice for this classic summer shell. This yarn has a high twist, which offers strong stitch definition to the knit work and minimizes the loft or bloom. Because the bloom is soft and minimal, the yarn gives the sweater loft without obscuring the cable twists. The yarn is forgiving, allowing the stitches to melt into place and making a fabric that looks like it is created from very uniformly knit stitches. Although a light color shows pattern work well, a medium color fares just as well here as the cable is not delicate or tiny. A darker color might hide the cabled design.

Often in cable work, knitters find that the purl stitches on either side of the cable panel tend to look looser than the main stitches of the cable pattern. When the yarn used has a soft bloom, as with the Super Taj Mahal, the bloom helps fill in the gaps, making for a much tighter and well-knit design.

Skill level: Intermediate ◼◼◼◻

Sizes: Women's XS (S, M, L, XL, 2X)

Finished bust: 32 (35, 39, 41, 46, 50)"

Finished length: 18½ (20, 20½, 22, 22½, 23)"

MATERIALS

4 (4, 5, 6, 7, 8) balls of Super Taj Mahal from Lane Cervinia (70% superfine merino, 22% silk, 8% cashmere; 50 g; 127 yds) in color 1422

Size 5 (3.75 mm) circular needle, 16" long, and size 5 straight needles

Size 6 (4 mm) circular needle, 16" long, and size 6 straight needles, or size needed to obtain gauge

Cable needle

Tapestry needle

GAUGE

22 sts = 4" in St st on size 6 needle.

CABLE PANEL

(Worked over 26 sts)

C4F: Sl next 2 sts onto cn and hold in front; K2, K2 from cn.

C4B: Sl next 2 sts onto cn and hold in back; K2, K2 from cn.

T3F: Sl next 2 sts onto cn and hold in front; P1, K2 from cn.

T3B: Sl next st onto cn and hold in back; K2, P1 from cn.

T4F: Sl next 2 sts onto cn and hold in front; P2, K2 from cn.

T4B: Sl next 2 sts onto cn and hold in back; K2, P2 from cn.

Rows 1 and 3 (WS): K3, P4, (K4, P4) twice, K3.

Row 2: P3, C4B, (P4, C4B) twice, P3.

Row 4: P2, T3B, (T4F, T4B) twice, T3F, P2.

Rows 5 and 15: K2, P2, K3, P4, K4, P4, K3, P2, K2.

Row 6: P1, T3B, P3, C4F, P4, C4B, P3, T3F, P1.

Rows 7 and 13: K1, P2, K4, (P4, K4) twice, P2, K1.

Row 8: P1, K2, P3, T3B, T4F, T4B, T3F, P3, K2, P1.

Rows 9 and 11: K1, (P2, K3) twice, P4, (K3, P2) twice, K1.

Row 10: P1, (K2, P3) twice, C4B, (P3, K2) twice, P1.

Row 12: P1, K2, P3, T3F, T4B, T4F, T3B, P3, K2, P1.

Row 14: P1, T3F, P3, C4F, P4, C4B, P3, T3B, P1.

Row 16: P2, T3F, (T4B, T4F) twice, T3B, P2.

Rep rows 1–16 for cable insert patt.

Knitting this garment is easier than it looks—it is mostly stockinette stitch finished with garter-stitch edgings. The only complexity is an intermediate-level cabled panel in the front.

BACK

With smaller straight needles, loosely CO 72 (80, 90, 98, 108, 116) sts and work in garter st for 6 rows. Change to larger straight needles, and working in St st, work side incs as follows: Inc 1 st at each end of every 8th row 6 (7, 6, 7, 7, 7) times, then inc 1 st at each end of every 10th row 0 (0, 2, 2, 3, 4) times—84 (94, 106, 116, 128, 138) sts.

Work even until work measures 11½ (12¾, 13, 14¼, 14½, 14¾)", ending with a WS row.

Armhole shaping: BO 7 sts at beg of next 2 rows, then BO 2 sts at beg of next 4 (6, 8, 10, 12, 14) rows, then dec 1 st at each end of EOR 5 (6, 8, 8, 9, 10) times—52 (56, 60, 66, 72, 76) sts. When piece measures 17¼ (18¾, 19¼, 20¾, 21¼, 21¾)" from beg, shape neck.

Neck shaping: BO 26 (26, 26, 28, 30, 30) center sts for neck and finish each side separately. At each neck edge on EOR, BO 2 sts twice, then 1 st 3 times.

When work measures 18½ (20, 20½, 22, 22½, 23)" from beg, BO rem 6 (8, 10, 12, 14, 16) sts for each shoulder.

FRONT

With smaller needles, loosely CO 72 (80, 90, 98, 108, 116) sts and work in garter st for 6 rows. Change to larger needles, knit 1 row.

Next row (WS): Beg patt as follows: Work across 23 (27, 32, 36, 41, 45) sts, pm, work row 1 of cable panel, pm, work across rem 23 (27, 32, 36, 41, 45) sts.

Cont cable panel on center 26 sts as est, and work side incs and armhole shaping as for back. When piece measures 15½ (17, 17½, 19, 19½, 20)" from beg, shape neck.

Neck shaping: BO the 26 (26, 26, 28, 30, 30) center sts for neck and finish each side separately as for back.

When work measures 18½ (20, 20½, 22, 22½, 23)" from beg, BO rem 6 (8, 10, 12, 14, 16) sts for each shoulder.

FINISHING

Join side and shoulder seams. With RS facing you and smaller circular needle, PU 98 (98, 100, 102, 104, 106) sts around neck and work 5 rnds in garter st (*purl 1 rnd, knit 1 rnd, rep from *). BO all sts. With RS facing you and smaller circular needle, PU 96 (98, 100, 102, 104, 106) sts around armhole and work 5 rnds in garter st as for neck. BO all sts. Rep for other armhole.

Weave in all ends. Block if desired.

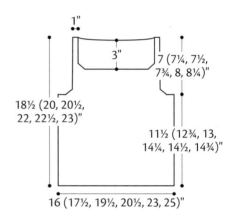

1"

3"

7 (7¼, 7½, 7¾, 8, 8¼)"

18½ (20, 20½, 22, 22½, 23)"

11½ (12¾, 13, 14¼, 14½, 14¾)"

16 (17½, 19½, 20½, 23, 25)"

Cable chart

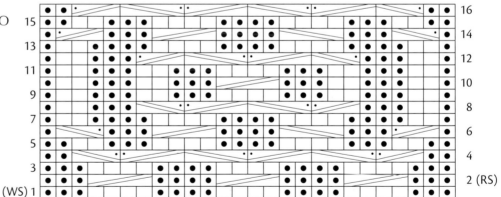

Key

☐ K on RS, P on WS

● P on RS, K on WS

◸ T3F: sl next 2 sts to cn and hold in front, P1, K2 from cn

◹ T3B: sl next st to cn and hold in back, K2, P1 from cn

◸ C4F: sl next 2 sts to cn and hold in front, K2, K2 from cn

◸ C4B: sl next 2 sts to cn and hold in back, K2, K2 from cn

◸ T4F: sl next 2 sts to cn and hold in front, P2, K2 from cn

◸ T4B: sl next 2 sts to cn and hold in back, K2, P2 from cn

ALTERNATE **PICKS** AND **PANS**

Here, JoAnne chose a mercerized cabled-construction cotton, which adds a hint of texture.  Mercerizing stretches and strengthens the fibers, giving yarn a beautiful sheen and deep and long-lasting colorations. The light brown color enhances the cabled design much better than a darker color would.

A GOOD CHOICE

Cotton has much less bloom than animal fibers, and the mercerizing process removes much of that bloom. The final yarn is shinier and is slicker and has very little elasticity. The cotton will not allow stitches to spring back into place to give the appearance of firmly knit stitches. Stitches knit with mercerized cotton may tend to look uneven, especially the purl stitches on each side of the cable panel.

The disappointment with the mercerized cotton was that the purl stitches along the side of the cable pattern need to be watched as you knit along. Be careful to allow for a uniform but not overly stretched look in the cable panel since this yarn is not as forgiving as animal fiber. With this yarn, only an experienced knitter can create a cable panel as uniform as the original garment.

Yarn: 3 (3, 3, 4, 4, 5) hanks of Butterfly Cotton from S R Kertzer (100% mercerized cotton; 125 g; 249 yds) in color 3307

Needles: Size 5 (3.75 mm) and size 6 (4 mm) circular needles, each16" long, and size 5 and 6 straight needles, or size required to obtain gauge

Knit in Butterfly from S R Kertzer

Knit in Fun from Cascade Yarns

A NOT-SO-GOOD CHOICE

Since there were no solid colors available in this yarn, JoAnne chose a marled-effect yarn, in which multiple strands of closely related shades of yarn are twisted together. Because of its high rayon content, the yarn has a nice sheen, but one of the plies is intentionally overtwisted, causing what's known as pigtails, when the overtwist of one ply causes it to twist back on itself in small areas, raising it from the rest of the yarn at regular intervals. Because this yarn is a cellulose fiber, it has no elasticity and no bloom. The marled effect and high texture detract from the cable, as does the very soft twist, which provides low stitch definition. This type of yarn shows off its own texture, not the texture of the cable panel.

Knit in Soft Sea Wool from Reynolds

FAUX-CABLE RIBBED SOCKS

By Donna Druchunas

These socks are quick and easy to make with a faux-cable ribbing pattern and DK-weight yarn. They are worked from the top down, with classic heel- and toe-shaping techniques. The ribbing keeps the leg and ankle snug, the heel stitch adds extra strength to an area that gets extra wear, and the stockinette stitch is smooth on the foot, making the socks quite comfortable to wear.

Because of the exaggerated twist of this yarn, the knit fabric is quite strong, and it also gives the stockinette-stitch portion of the sock an interesting texture. If you have extra-sensitive feet, try working the foot of the sock inside out so that the smooth knit side of the fabric is on the inside and the bumpy purl stitches are on the outside. You can also work in a tighter gauge than is normally recommended for the chosen yarn to add strength and make the fabric smoother and more comfortable.

Skill level: Intermediate ◼◼◼◻

Sizes: Women's S (M, L)

Foot Circumference: Approx 6 (6¾, 7½)" around foot

MATERIALS

2 skeins of Soft Sea Wool from Reynolds (100% wool; 50 g; 162 yds/147 m) in color 0514 Pale blue

Size 4 (3.5 mm) double-pointed needles, or size needed to obtain gauge

Size 3 (3.25 mm) double-pointed needles

Stitch holder

Tapestry needle

GAUGE

26 sts = 4" in St st using large needles

PATTERN STITCHES

K2, P2 Ribbing

(Multiple of 4 sts)

All rnds: *K2, P2; rep from * around.

Faux Cable Ribbing

(Multiple of 4 sts)

Rnds 1–3: *K2, P2; rep from * around.

Rnd 4: *K2tog, leaving both sts on needle; then insert RH needle between the 2 sts just knit tog, and knit first st again; then sl both sts to RH needle tog, P2; rep from * around.

SOCK (MAKE 2)

Sl all sts as if to purl unless other instructed.

With smaller needles, CO 40 (44, 48) sts. Arrange sts on 3 dpns, and join to work in rnd, being careful not to twist sts.

Work in K2, P2 ribbing for 1".

Change to larger needles, work in faux cable ribbing until leg measures approx 5" from CO edge. Work 1 (0, 1) more st onto same needle to center ribbing patt on heel.

Heel

Knit across 20 (22, 24) sts and put these sts on holder for instep.

Place rem 20 (22, 24) sts onto 1 dpn for heel.

Faux cables can dress up sock ribbing and are much easier to knit than actual cables.

Heel Flap

(Worked back and forth)

Row 1 (RS): *Sl 1 wyib, K1; rep from * to end of heel sts.

Row 2 (WS): Sl 1 wyif, purl to end of heel sts.

Rep rows 1 and 2 until heel is a square. End after completing row 2.

Turn Heel

Row 1 (RS): Knit across 12 (13, 14) sts, ssk, K1, turn work.

Row 2: Sl 1, P5, P2tog, P1 turn.

Row 3: Sl 1, knit to 1 st before gap, ssk, K1, turn.

Row 4: Sl 1, purl to 1 st before gap, P2tog, P1, turn.

Rep rows 3 and 4 until all heel sts have been worked. End after a WS row.

Heel Gusset

Knit across all heel sts.

Needle 1: PU 1 st in each slipped st along side edge of heel flap.

Needle 2: Work across instep sts, maintaining baby cable ribbing patt.

Needle 3: PU 1 st in each slipped st along side edge of heel flap, knit half of the heel sts.

Note that number of sts will vary depending how on many rows you worked for the heel flap. Don't worry about this. The extra sts will be dec as you work the instep.

Instep

Return to working in rnd.

Rnd 1:

Needle 1: Knit to last 3 sts, K2tog, K1.

Needle 2: Work across all sts on instep in est patt.

Needle 3: K1, ssk, knit to end—2 sts dec.

Rnd 2: Work even in est patt (faux cable ribbing on instep, St st on rem sts).

Rep rnds 1 and 2 until 40 (44, 48) sts rem.

Foot

Work even in est patt until foot measures 5 (5½, 6)" from back of heel, or until foot is 1½" shorter than desired length.

Toe

Rnd 1:

Needle 1: Knit to last 3 sts, K2tog, K1.

Needle 2: K1, ssk, knit to last 3 sts, K2tog, K1.

Needle 3: K1, ssk, knit to end—4 sts dec.

Rnd 2: Knit.

Rep rnds 1 and 2 until 16 sts rem.

Knit sts from needle 1 onto needle 3—8 sts on each needle.

Cut yarn, leaving a 12" tail. Join toe with kitchener st.

Weave in ends.

ALTERNATE PICKS AND PANS

For this version, Donna tried a wool/acrylic blend yarn that is incredibly soft and spun with a looser twist than a traditional sock yarn. The soft yarn feels wonderful and still shows the stitch pattern beautifully. These socks make you feel like you're walking on a cloud. If you choose a soft yarn that is 100% wool, you can add a carry-along nylon thread when knitting the heel and toe for added strength.

Because of the high acrylic content of these socks, they may not be comfortable in warm weather or inside heavy shoes because they won't breathe as freely or wick moisture away from your skin as well as pure wool fiber would. Consider wearing these socks in bed or as slippers for cuddly warmth in the winter months.

Yarn: 2 balls of Cashsoft Baby DK from Rowan Classic Yarns (57% extra-fine merino, 33% microfiber, 10% cashmere; 50 g; 142 yds/130 m) in color SH03 Peach

Needles: Size 4 (3.5 mm) and size 3 (3.25 mm) double-pointed needles, or size needed to obtain gauge

> A GOOD CHOICE

Knit in Cashsoft Baby DK from Rowan Classic Yarns

Knit in Carezza from Adriafil

> A NOT-SO-GOOD CHOICE

The final yarn Donna tried for the socks is an angora, polyester, and wool blend. It has a very soft twist and is a little furry. The pattern stitch doesn't show up as well in the furry yarn as it does in a smoother yarn, but the main problem with these socks is that they would probably get holes after just a few wearings. The yarn is designed to be soft and comfy, not hard wearing. Socks knit in this yarn would, however, make a wonderful gift for someone who is bedridden or for a new mother who needs some luxurious slippers to keep her toes warm when she gets to sit down and rest her feet for a few moments.

WORSTED-WEIGHT YARN

Worsted is the most common fiber weight and as popular as it is ubiquitous. Skein for skein, knitters get a lot of mileage from worsted-weight yarn and it's likely that a large part of anyone's stash contains this weight fiber, whether it was picked up at a sale or is leftover from a large project. Worsted-weight yarn comes in a myriad of fibers, textures, and colors, and knits quickly on medium to large needles. Because this yarn is thick and easy to handle, even beginner knitters can let their designer sides shine.

With so much to choose from in the worsted category, substitution possibilities are endless. However, it is easy to pick too many yarns or to choose yarns that do not knit well together. But avoiding these pitfalls is easy, and we are here to show you how.

SIDE-TO-SIDE SWEATER

SELF-STRIPING VEST

ARAN VEST

MOSAIC JACKET

Knit in Potluck Worsted and accented with
Possum Worsted, both from Cherry Tree Hill Yarn

SIDE-TO-SIDE SWEATER

By Cheryl Potter

Side-to-side sweaters are most often worked from cuff to cuff. When variegated yarns are used, they're usually the self-striping variety to provide vertical interest that is also figure flattering. For this sweater, I used Potluck yarn, which is dyed randomly rather than in a repeated pattern. It tends to give garments a more artistic and whimsical look and works well in vertical knitting. This yarn is combined with solid-colored Possum yarn to create evenly spaced vertical stripes of color that help balance the more random (and sometimes concentrated) sections of Potluck color. The differences in texture between the smooth Potluck yarn and fuzzy Possum is appealing and makes the exotic Possum stand out.

What may surprise the knitter is that this side-to-side sweater has a secret seam hidden by one of the garter ridges in both the front and back. The sweater is knit in two pieces, each from the sleeve cuff to the center of the body. The pieces are then joined using the three-needle-bind-off technique in the center of one of the garter-ridge rows, creating an invisible secret bind off.

Skill level: Intermediate ■■■□

Sizes: S (M, L, XL)

Finished bust: 41 (44, 47, 50)"

Finished length: 24 (24 1/2, 25½, 26)"

MATERIALS

MC 2 (3, 3, 4) hanks of Potluck Worsted from Cherry Tree Hill Yarn (100% wool; 4 oz; 280 yds) in Potluck color family of blues/purples

CC 6 (6, 7, 8) skeins of Possum Worsted from Cherry Tree Hill Yarn (80% wool, 20% possum; 50 g; 109 yds) in color Eggplant

Size 5 (3.75 mm) circular needles, 16" and 29" long

Size 7 (4.5 mm) circular needles, 16" and 29" long, or size needed to obtain gauge

1 stitch marker

Tapestry needle

GAUGE

8 sts and 20 rows = 4" in St st on larger needles

STOCKINETTE-STITCH AND GARTER-RIDGE PATTERN

Rows 1–7 (WS): Starting with purl row, and using MC, work in St st. Break yarn.

Rows 8–10: Using CC, knit all rows.

Rep rows 1–10 for patt.

The sweater is knit in two pieces, from the left sleeve to the center, and then from the right sleeve to the center. The sleeves and body are worked in stockinette-stitch and garter-ridge pattern throughout.

LEFT PIECE

With smaller needle and CC, CO 36 (38, 40, 42) sts.

Cuff

Beg with purl row, work in St st for 6 rows, ending with a RS row.

Next row (WS): Knit to form a garter ridge.

Knit 1 row. Purl 1 row.

Next row (RS): Purl to form a garter ridge.

Purl 1 row. Knit 1 row.

Next row (WS): Knit to form a garter ridge.

Next row: Knit, inc 4 (6, 8, 12) sts evenly across row—40 (44, 48, 54) sts. Break yarn.

Sleeve

Change to 16" long size 7 circular needle, attach MC, and beg 10-row St-st and garter-ridge patt on WS, while AT SAME TIME work incs as given below. Change to 29" long size 7 circular needle as needed.

Sleeve increases: While working in est patt, inc 1 st on each side every third row 20 times, then every fourth row 3 times—86 (90, 94, 100) sts.

Cont even total length is approx 17", ending with row 7 of patt. (Adjust sleeve length here if needed, making note of what row you are ending on so that the other sleeve can be made the same. End with row 7 of the patt.) Break yarn.

Body

Cont in patt as est, and leaving sleeve sts on LH needle, attach CC and use cable CO on page 00 to CO 56 (56, 58, 58) sts on RH needle for back, work across back sts, work 43 (45, 47, 50) sts of sleeve in est patt, pm (shoulder seam), work rem sleeve sts. Turn and use cable CO to CO 56 (56, 58, 58) sts for front—198 (202, 210, 216) sts.

Cont even in patt as est until body measures 6¾ (7½, 8, 9)".

Front Neck Shaping

Cont patt as est, working back and front at same time using 2 balls of yarn.

Row 1 (RS): Work to marker, remove marker. With a second ball of yarn, BO 2 sts, work to end of row.

Rows 2, 4, and 6 (WS): Work to 2 sts before front neck edge, dec 1 st.

Row 3: At neck edge, BO 2 sts.

Row 5: At neck edge, BO 3 sts.

Row 7: At neck edge, BO 3 sts.

Row 8: As row 2.

Cont in est patt until front piece measures approx 10¼ (11, 11¾, 12½)", ending with row 8 of patt.

Place left side sts on a spare needle, set aside.

RIGHT PIECE

With smaller needles and CC, CO 36 (38, 40, 42) sts.

Cuff

Beg with purl row, work in St st for 6 rows, ending with a RS row.

Next row (WS): Knit to form a ridge. Knit 1 row. Purl 1 row.

Next row (RS): Purl to form a ridge. Purl 1 row. Knit 1 row.

Next row (WS): Knit to form a ridge.

Next row: Knit, inc 4 (6, 8, 12) sts evenly across row—40 (44, 48, 54) sts. Break yarn.

Sleeve

Change to 16" long size 7 circular needle, attach MC, and beg 10-row St-st and garter-ridge patt on WS, while AT SAME TIME work incs as given below. Change to 29" long size 7 circular needle as needed.

Sleeve increases: While working in est patt, inc 1 st on each side every third row 20 times, then every fourth row 3 times—86 (90, 94, 100) sts.

Cont even total length is approx 17", ending with row 7 of patt. (Adjust sleeve length here if needed, making note of what row you are ending on so that the other sleeve can be made the same. End with row 7 of the patt.) Break yarn.

Body

Cont in patt as est, and leaving sleeve sts on LH needle, attach CC and use cable CO to CO 56 (56, 58, 58) sts on RH needle for front, work across front sts, work 43 (45, 47, 50) sts of sleeve in est patt, pm (center of shoulder), work rem sleeve sts. Turn and use cable CO to CO 56 (56, 58, 58) sts for back—198 (202, 210, 216) sts.

Cont even in patt as est until body measures 6¾ (7½, 8, 9)".

Front Neck Shaping

Cont in est patt, working back and front at the same time using 2 balls of yarn.

Row 1 (WS): Work to marker, remove marker. With a second ball of yarn, BO 2 sts, work to end of row.

Rows 2, 4, and 6 (RS): Work to 2 sts before front neck edge, dec 1 st.

Row 3: At neck edge, BO 2 sts.

Row 5: At neck edge, BO 3 sts.

Row 7: At neck edge, BO 3 sts.

Row 8: As row 2.

Cont in est patt until front piece measures approx 10¼ (11, 11¾, 12½)", ending with row 8 of patt.

Leave sts on needle.

FINISHING

Using CC, and with WS sides tog, join the two halves of front and back with 3-needle BO; this will make a ridge on the RS. Sew side seams and sleeve seams.

Body border: With smaller 29" circular needle and CC, PU 184 sts evenly around bottom edge. Join and pm. Knit 2 rnds, purl 1 rnd, knit 2 rnds, purl 1 rnd, knit 6 rnds. BO loosely.

Neck border: With smaller 16" circular needle and CC, PU 76 (84, 84, 88) sts around neck edge. Join and pm. Knit 2 rnds, purl 1 rnd, knit 2 rnds, purl 1 rnd, knit 6 rnds. BO loosely.

Weave in all ends. Block lightly.

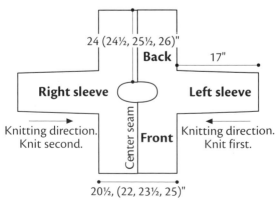

24 (24½, 25½, 26)"
Back
17"
Right sleeve
Left sleeve
Center seam
Front
Knitting direction. Knit second.
Knitting direction. Knit first.
20½, (22, 23½, 25)"

ALTERNATE **PICKS** AND **PANS**

For this version, I used a fuzzy angora yarn that is technically DK-weight instead of worsted, but because the angora is so lofty, it knits to worsted-weight gauge. The coordinating Brown Sheep yarn is space dyed in a colorway called Blueberry Hill which contains the teal color, making the coordination with the solid teal angora pleasing.

A GOOD CHOICE

Knit in hand-painted Lamb's Pride Worsted from Brown Sheep Company and Soft Angora from Cherry Tree Hill Yarn

Yarn:

MC 3 (4, 4, 5) skeins of Lamb's Pride Worsted from Brown Sheep Company (85% wool, 15% mohair; 4 oz; 190 yds) hand painted by Cherry Tree Hill Yarn in colorway Blueberry Hill

CC 6 (6, 7, 8) skeins of Soft Angora from Cherry Tree Hill Yarn (80% wool, 20% angora; 50 g; 109 yds) in color Teal

Needles: 2 size 5 (3.75 mm) circular needles, 16" and 29" long, and 2 size 7 (4.5 mm) circular needles, 16" and 29" long, or size needed to obtain gauge

Knit in Rayon Bouclé and Baby Sachet, both from Cherry Tree Hill Yarn

A NOT-SO-GOOD CHOICE

For this swatch, I used a worsted-weight textured rayon and a worsted-weight ribbon to make a garment to wear during the transition from winter to spring. Both yarns are hand painted in the same colorway. As you can see, the colorways merge together instead of creating contrast, so the interest of the vertical ridge in the garter pattern is lost. The resultant sweater may be overly gaudy.

In addition, both of these yarns tend to stretch vertically. Since this sweater is knit from side to side, and because of the characteristics of rayon and ribbon, this garment will grow wider and wider and stretch out of shape with each wearing. It would have been better to use one yarn that would temper the other—for example, if you'd like to use ribbon as a highlight, it's best to pair it with a yarn that has memory and less stretch. Used in a traditionally horizontally knit garment, there would be no stretch and the garment would work out fine.

Knit in Colorspun Worsted from
Plymouth Yarn Company

SELF-STRIPING VEST

By JoAnne Turcotte

Self-striping yarns are a wonderful new invention for the knitter, but not all patterns will be successful with these yarns. This vest pattern, knit in one piece to the armholes, works because the Colorspun yarn exhibits a long striping pattern, called a drifting stripe, which is longer and more subtle than the Boku (discussed in "A Good Choice" on page 59). In the Colorspun, the stripes change at very long intervals of about 4 yards and only two of the four plies stripe. While this may not be the best self-striping yarn to use for multi-directional knitting, where intense, sharp, quick color changes cause the most excitement, it does a very good job of producing a pleasant-looking garment constructed in one easy piece.

The wide area at the bottom shows thinner stripes than the top. As the knitting changes to the shorter areas of the upper front and upper back, the striping widens but the longer sections of color in the colorspun drift slowly, which is more soothing to the eye than in the Boku vest.

Skill level: Easy ◀■□□

Sizes: Women's S (M, L, XL)

Finished bust: 36 (40, 44, 48)"

Finished length: 20 (21, 22, 22)"

MATERIALS

4 (5, 5, 6) skeins of Encore Colorspun Worsted from Plymouth Yarn Company (75% acrylic, 25% wool; 100 g; 200 yds) in color 7172

Size 6 (4 mm) circular needle, 24" or 29" long

Size 7 (4.5 mm) circular needle, 24" or 29" long, or size needed to obtain gauge

Tapestry needle

4 buttons, approx 7/8" diameter

GAUGE

18 sts and 22 rows = 4" in St st using larger needles

VEST

Vest is worked in 1 piece to the armholes.

With smaller needle, CO 166 (182, 198, 214) sts.

Knit 4 rows.

Next row (first buttonhole): K3, YO, K2tog, knit to end of row.

Knit 5 more rows.

Change to larger needle and cont as follows:

Row 1 (RS): Knit.

Row 2 (WS): K5, purl to last 5 sts, K5.

Rep rows 1 and 2 until piece measures 10½", end by working a RS row, AT SAME TIME make a buttonhole every 3½" on a RS row as above until there are a total of 4 buttonholes.

Next row (WS): K5, P24 (28, 32, 36), K26, P56 (64, 72, 80), K26, P24 (28, 32, 36), K5.

Next row (RS): Knit.

Rep last 2 rows twice, and then the first row again, keeping continuity of buttonholes.

Divide for armholes (RS): K34 (38, 42, 46) for right front, BO 16 sts, K66 (74, 82, 90) for back, BO 16 sts, K34 (38, 42, 46) for left front.

Left front: Working on first (34, 38, 42, 46) sts, cont as follows:

Row 1: K5, purl to last 5 sts, K5.

Row 2: Knit to last 7 sts, K2tog, K5.

Row 3: As row 1.

Row 4: Knit.

Rep rows 1–4 a total of 11 times—23 (27, 31, 35) sts.

Rep rows 3 and 4 until armhole measures 9½ (10½, 11½, 11½)", ending with a WS row. Place all sts on a holder for 3-needle BO.

Back: Reattach yarn and work across next 66 (74, 82, 90) sts for back as follows:

Row 1: K5, purl to last 5 sts, K5.

Row 2: Knit.

Rep last 2 rows until armhole measures 7½ (8½, 9½, 9½)".

Next row: K5, P13 (17, 21, 25), K30, P13 (17, 21, 25), K5.

Next row: Knit.

Rep last 2 rows until total length is same as front.

Place all sts on a holder for 3-needle BO.

Right front: Reattach yarn and work across rem 34 (38, 42, 46) sts as follows:

Row 1: K5, purl to last 5 sts, K5.

Row 2: K5, ssk, knit to end.

Row 3: As row 1.

Row 4: Knit.

Rep rows 1–4 a total of 11 times—23 (27, 31, 35) sts.

Rep rows 3 and 4 until armhole measures 9½ (10½, 11½, 11½)", ending with a WS row. Place all sts on a holder for 3-needle BO.

FINISHING

Join shoulder seams tog using 3-needle BO. Sew buttons to correspond with buttonholes. Weave in all ends. Block lightly.

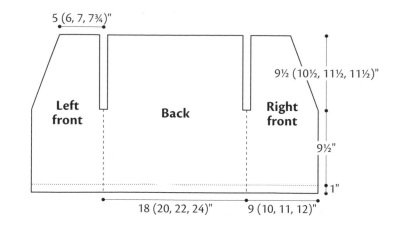

ALTERNATE **PICKS** AND **PANS**

The stripes in Boku are shorter than in Colorspun. This makes very thin stripes until the underarms are reached, where the garment is split into three pieces: the right front, back, and left front. After the split, the striping pattern is worked over half of the stitches for the back and a quarter of the stitches for each front.

A GOOD CHOICE

The width of the stripes changes and varies for the different sections of the top of the vest. While the logical solution would be to find two balls of the yarn that look alike and use them for the fronts, it may not be possible at this point in time because much of the yarn has been used. This yarn does exhibit a repeatable pattern—while the stripes at the bottom are thinner, the wider stripes at the top are still repeatable and do work, even though they aren't the same.

This garment was knit using random balls of yarn and the two front-top areas have different colors showing. Planning the garment and saving two matching balls from the beginning may have been the answer here if you want your garment to have matching sides.

Yarn: 8 (9,10,11) skeins of Boku from Plymouth Yarn (95% wool, 5% silk; 50g, 99 yds) in color 9

Needles: Size 6 (4 mm) and size 7 (4.5 mm) circular needles, 24" or 29" long, or size needed to obtain gauge.

Knit in Boku from Plymouth Yarn Company

Knit in Bewitched
from Plymouth Yarn Company

A NOT-SO-GOOD CHOICE

Bewitched is a unique mixed-material yarn that stripes in a long length and non-repeating pattern. Each color and texture changes to another after approximately 1 to 2 yards. Some stripes are longer, some are shorter, but basically the stripes changes randomly as the yarn is comprised of up to 20 different yarn types. This will be an unusable yarn for any pattern where sections need to be matched. Although striping yarn is popular, it does not work with a pattern that changes fabric width as drastically as this one does, and does not repeat. This yarn would work well with a large repeat that does not depend upon a certain stripe like a large shawl or coat or jacket knit in one piece.

Knit in Lamb's Pride Worsted from Brown Sheep Company

ARAN VEST

by Donna Druchunas

Donna has been enamored of Aran knitting ever since her grandmother made her what she called an Iris pattern sweater in the 1970s. Here, in her updated version of an Aran vest, Donna incorporates three of her favorite stitches: honeycomb cables, braid cables, and moss stitch. There are also two options for the back. Option 1 is knit in moss stitch to work up quickly and to be less bulky and warm than a fully cabled version. Option 2 matches the cable patterns on the front and requires an extra ball of yarn.

Although this yarn has "worsted" in its name and it fits into the worsted category, it is actually slightly heavier than a standard worsted-weight yarn and works up at a gauge of 4½ stitches per inch. For this vest, the yarn created a firm fabric that allowed the cable patterns to pop.

The yarn is composed of 100%-wool singles (or unplied) yarn with a smooth texture and a solid color. Because the yarn is a single, however, if the back is worked in plain moss stitch, the fabric will twist diagonally, and will require a lot of blocking before sewing the vest together. Steaming the piece through a damp towel should help it hold its shape even after future washing.

Skill level: Intermediate ◼◼◼☐

Sizes: Women's S (M, L)

Finished bust: 37 (39, 41)"

Finished length: 23½ (24, 25)"

MATERIALS

4 (4, 5)* skeins of Lamb's Pride Worsted from Brown Sheep Company (85% wool, 15% mohair; 4 oz/113 g; 190 yds/173 m) in color M-109 Jaded Dreams

Size 6 (4 mm) needles, or size needed to obtain gauge

Size 4 (3.5 mm) needles

Stitch holders

Tapestry needle

Add 1 extra skein for optional cabled back on page 62.

GAUGE

18 sts and 20 rows = 4" over moss st using larger needles

MOSS STITCH

(Even number of sts)

Row 1 (RS): *K1, P1, rep from * to end of row.

Rows 2 and 4: Knit the knit sts and purl the purl sts as they face you.

Row 3: *P1, K1, rep from * to end of row.

Rep rows 1–4 for patt.

FRONT

With smaller needle, CO 78 (82, 86) sts.

Beg ribbing on RS row as follows: *K2, P2; rep from * to last 2 sts, K2.

Work in K2, P2 ribbing for 1". End after working a RS row.

Knit 2 rows.

Next row (WS): Knit, inc 20 (24, 24) sts evenly across—98 (106, 110) sts.

Set up patts: Change to larger needles and work 14 (14, 16) sts in moss st, work braid cable (chart 1 on page 62) over next 19 sts, work honeycomb cable (chart 2 on page 62) over next 32 (40, 40) sts, work braid cable over next 19 sts, work 14 (14, 16) sts in moss st.

Cont working patts as est until piece measures 14½ (15, 15½)" from beg. End after working a WS row.

Armhole shaping:

BO 4 sts at beg of next 2 rows—90 (98, 102) sts.

BO 3 sts at beg of next 2 rows—84 (92, 96) sts.

BO 2 sts at beg of next 2 (2, 4) rows—80 (88, 88) sts.

Dec 1 st at both ends of next 5 RS rows—70 (78, 78) sts.

The honeycomb and braided cables are accented by moss stitches.

Neck shaping: Work 25 (25, 25) sts in patts, BO center 20 (28, 28) sts, attach another skein of yarn, work rem 25 (25, 25) sts in patts as est. Work both sides at once. BO 2 sts at each neck edge EOR 3 times—19 sts in each shoulder.

Cont in patt st until piece measures 23½ (24, 25)". Place shoulder sts on holders.

BACK OPTION 1: PLAIN MOSS STITCH

Ribbing: With smaller needle, CO 78 (82, 86) sts.

Beg ribbing on RS row as follows: *K2, P2; rep from * to last 2 sts, K2.

Work in K2, P2 ribbing until ribbing measures 1". End after working a RS row.

Knit 2 rows.

Next row (WS): Knit, inc 6 sts evenly across—84 (88, 92) sts.

Change to larger needles and work in moss st until piece measures 14½ (15, 15½)" from beg. End after working a WS row.

Armhole shaping:

BO 4 sts at beg of next 2 rows—76 (80, 84) sts.

BO 3 sts at beg of next 2 rows—70 (74, 78) sts.

BO 2 sts at beg of next 2 (2, 4) rows—66 (70, 70) sts.

Dec 1 st at both ends of the next 5 RS rows—56 (60, 60) sts.

Cont in patt st until piece measures 23½ (24, 25)".

Do not BO. Place sts on holder.

BACK OPTION 2: CABLED BACK

Work as for front, omitting neck shaping. Do not BO.

FINISHING

Block pieces to measurements. Join shoulders with 3-needle BO. BO center back neck sts. Sew side seams.

Armhole edging: With RS facing you, starting at bottom of armhole and with smaller needles, PU 86 (86, 90) sts around armhole edge. Join and pm. Purl 1 row. Knit 1 row. Purl 1 row. Work in K2, P2 ribbing for 4 rows. BO loosely in patt.

Neckband: With RS facing you, starting at left shoulder seam and with smaller circular needle, PU 94 (98, 98) sts around neck edge. Join and pm. Purl 1 row. Knit 1 row. Purl 1 row. Work in K2, P2 ribbing for 4 rows. BO loosely in patt.

Weave in ends. Block lightly if desired.

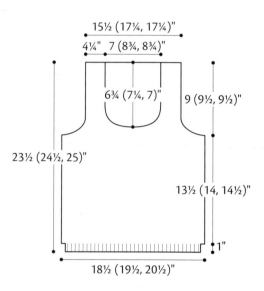

15½ (17¼, 17¼)"
4¼" 7 (8¾, 8¾)"
6¾ (7¼, 7)"   9 (9½, 9½)"
23½ (24½, 25)"
13½ (14, 14½)"
1"
18½ (19½, 20½)"

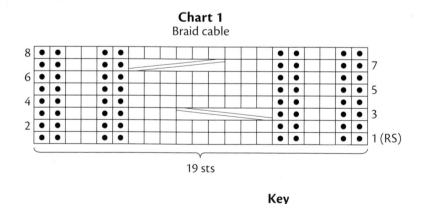

Chart 1
Braid cable

8
6
4
2
7
5
3
1 (RS)

19 sts

Chart 2
Honeycomb cable

8
6
4
2
7
5
3
1 (RS)

Work 8-st repeat
4 (5, 5) times.

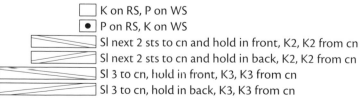

Key

☐ K on RS, P on WS
● P on RS, K on WS
Sl next 2 sts to cn and hold in front, K2, K2 from cn
Sl next 2 sts to cn and hold in back, K2, K2 from cn
Sl 3 to cn, hold in front, K3, K3 from cn
Sl 3 to cn, hold in back, K3, K3 from cn

ALTERNATE **PICKS** AND **PANS**

The cotton/wool blend used for this version is a true worsted-weight yarn, which typically is worked at 5 stitches per inch. Here, Donna used needles to get 4½ stitches per inch to match the gauge of the wool vest. The yarn is plied and will not twist or slant, even when the plain back option is chosen.

Knit in Cotton Fleece from Brown Sheep Company

A GOOD CHOICE

While the yarn has good stitch definition necessary for textured knitting, the cables and moss stitch are a little looser than with the wool yarn. Because this yarn has a large percentage of cotton, it may stretch out of shape with repeated washings.

Yarn: 4 (4, 5)* skeins of Cotton Fleece from Brown Sheep Company (80% pima cotton, 20% wool; 3.5 oz/100 g; 215 yds/197 m) in color CW-930 Candy Apple

*Add 1 extra skein for optional cabled back on page 62.

Needles: Size 6 (4 mm) and size 4 (3.5 mm) needles, or size needed to obtain gauge

Knit in 1824 Cotton
from Mission Falls

A NOT-SO-GOOD CHOICE

This cotton is machine washable and dryable, making for an easy-care vest. However, its pebbly texture doesn't allow the cable patterns to pop the way they do when knit with smooth yarns. Although it is possible to knit cables in textured yarn, the cables will compete with the yarn texture for attention. This yarn is so nicely textured that cables are not necessary to create interest.

Knit in Boku from Plymouth Yarn Company

MOSAIC JACKET

By Celeste Pinheiro

The design of this jacket lets you have fun experimenting with color that travels in different directions. The wool-blend yarn keeps the jacket in shape, gives nice drape, and provides a plethora of colors to play with.

The look of the jacket depends on some sort of striping to show off the different directions of the knitting. Celeste chose Boku from Plymouth Yarn Company for this version because of its hand-painted look combined with long stripes of color. The yarn is also smooth and even, with nothing to distract from the beautiful color play. The exciting part is that you don't know quite what colors each square will be until you knit them.

The jacket construction breaks up the stripes into a nice mosaic pattern. Because the design calls for large square motifs, you don't have to pick up many individual squares or sew a myriad of seams. The design looks more complicated than it is, and the knitting goes more quickly than you'd imagine.

Skill level: Intermediate ◼◼◼◻

Sizes: Women's S (M, L, 1X, 2X, 3X)

Finished bust: 38 (41, 44, 49, 52, 54)"

Finished length: 21 (22½, 24, 26½, 28, 29)"

MATERIALS

Boku from Plymouth Yarn Company (95% wool, 5% silk; 50 g; 99 yds)

1 4 (4, 5, 5, 6, 6) skeins in color 1

2 6 (7, 7, 8, 9, 10) skeins in color 2

3 2 (2, 3, 3, 3, 4) skeins (for cuffs and bands only) in color 3

Size 6 (4 mm) needles

Size 8 (5 mm) needles, or size needed to obtain gauge

Tapestry needle

3 buttons, approx 1" diameter

GAUGE

18 sts = 4" in St st using larger needles

JACKET

The jacket body is made of 3 A squares and 3 B squares, plus 1 partial A and 1 partial B square at the front neck. The sleeves are knit down from the shoulders. The hem is picked up and knit after sewing the front and back tog.

Referring to the stripe sequence chart below, knit squares for version 1 in alternating stripes of color 1 and color 2, and squares for version 2 as indicated by letters A–K on the chart. See sidebar on page 67 for additional instructions for version 2.

Stripe sequence

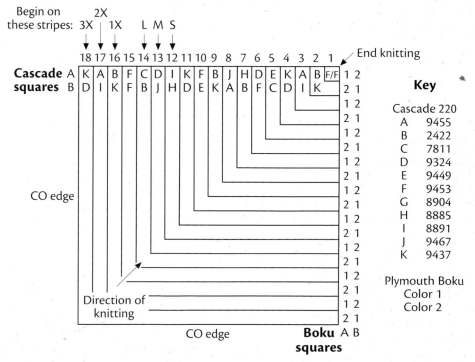

Key

Cascade 220

A	9455
B	2422
C	7811
D	9324
E	9449
F	9453
G	8904
H	8885
I	8891
J	9467
K	9437

Plymouth Boku
Color 1
Color 2

Knitting the mitered squares is a fun exercise in color play.

SQUARE PATTERN

Rows 1, 3, and 5 (RS): With larger needles, knit.

Rows 2 and 4 (WS): Purl.

Row 6: Change to smaller needles, change yarn and knit.

Rep rows 1–6 and work in colors as indicated. Work decs as indicated in basic square.

BASIC SQUARE FOR BODY

With first yarn, CO 87 (93, 99, 111, 117, 123) sts. This includes 1 st at each side for selvages.

Purl 1 row (WS); this is not part of the square patt.

Working in 6-row square patt as shown above, dec 2 sts on EOR as follows:

Row 1 (RS): K42 (45, 48, 54, 57, 60), sl 1 kw-K2tog-psso, K42 (45, 48, 54, 57, 60).

Row 2: Purl.

Row 3: K41 (44, 47, 53, 56, 59), sl 1 kw-K2tog-psso, knit to end.

Cont in square patt as est, and dec 2 sts on EOR as above until 21 total sts rem, end with row 2 of square patt.

Now dec every row, working decs on RS as above, and work dec on WS as follows: sl 3 sts kw one at a time to RH needle, sl 3 sts back to LH needle and P3tog tbl. Cont dec on every row, do not change yarn again, and cont working in St st until 3 sts rem. Pull tail through sts.

PARTIAL SQUARES FOR NECK

Make 1 each of A and B squares.

Work as given for basic square until 45 (45, 45, 51, 51, 51) total sts rem, ending with a RS row. BO all sts on WS.

JOINING SQUARES

Sew squares tog for front and back according to diagram below. Sew shoulder seams.

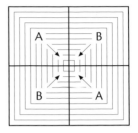

Back

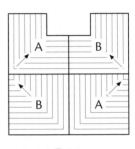

Front

SLEEVES

Pm 8 (8½, 9, 9½, 10, 10½)" down from shoulder on back and front. With RS facing you and using color 1, PU 74 (79, 83, 87, 92, 97) sts between markers.

Next row (WS): Purl.

Work in square patt, AT SAME TIME on row 5 of st patt and every 6 (6, 6, 4, 4, 4) rows after that, dec 1 st at each side 17 (17, 17, 20, 20, 21) times—40 (45, 49, 47, 52, 55) sts.

Work until 15 (15, 15, 14, 14, 14)" from pick up, ending on row 5 of square patt.

Cuff: Change to smaller needles, and using color 3, cont in garter st and work until sleeve measures 17 (17, 17, 16, 16, 16)" from beg. BO all sts

FINISHING

Hem: With RS facing you, smaller needles, and color 3, PU 176 (188, 200, 224, 236, 245) sts, this includes 1 selvage st at each side. Work in garter st until 2" from pick up. BO all sts.

Neck band: With RS facing you, smaller needles, and color 3, PU 44 (44, 44, 50, 50, 50) sts along right neck (you are picking up 1 st for each bound-off st of square plus the 1 selvage st), PU 35 (35, 35, 44, 44, 44) sts along back neck, PU 44 (44, 44, 50, 50, 50) sts along left neck edge. Knit 1 row. Beg dec on next RS row as follows: K21 (21, 21, 24, 24, 24), sl 1 kw-K2tog-psso, K75 (75, 75, 90, 90, 90), sl 1 kw-K2tog-psso, knit to end (you are cont decs of partial squares). Knit 14 more rows, making 2 dec EOR as est. BO all sts.

Button band: With RS facing you, smaller needles, and color 3, PU 82 (88, 95, 106, 113, 117) sts along left front. Knit 9 rows, BO all sts

Buttonhole band: With RS facing you, smaller needles, and using color 3, PU sts as for button band along right front. Knit 7 rows. Work buttonhole row as follows: K52 (58, 65, 73, 80, 84), [BO 3, K9 (9, 9, 11, 11, 11)] twice, BO 3, K3. Next buttonhole row: Knit, CO 3 sts over BO sts of previous row. BO all sts.

Closure: Sew buttons opposite buttonholes along pickup row.

INSTRUCTIONS FOR VERSION 2

See photo of version 2 on page 69.

Refer to stripe sequence chart on page 65 to make basic squares. Follow instructions for version 1 as given above with the following exceptions:

Sleeves: Work stripe sequence as follows: *H, E, K, A, F, C, I, K, F, J; rep from * as needed.

Cuff: Change to smaller needles, knit 8 rows in G, 3 rows in J, 3 rows in H, and 5 rows in C. BO all sts.

Hem: PU sts and work as for version 1, following color sequence as for version 2 cuff.

Neck band: PU sts and work as for version 1 in following color sequence: PU sts with G and knit 4 rows, knit 3 rows in J, knit 3 rows in H, knit 3 rows in C. BO all sts.

Button band: PU sts as for version 1 using C and knit 6 rows, knit 3 rows in F. BO all sts.

Buttonhole band: With RS facing you, smaller needles, and using color G, PU as for button band along right front and knit 6 rows. Knit 1 row in H. Work RS and WS buttonhole rows as for version 1. BO all sts.

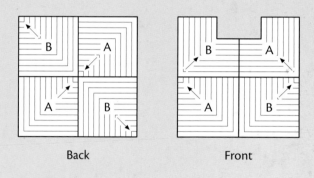

Back   Front

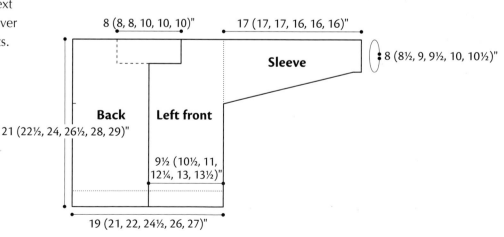

ALTERNATE **PICKS** AND **PANS**

For this version, Celeste used 11 different
colors to show how you can successfully
stitch this pattern using odd balls of yarn. Although plainer than
the original, the Cascade Yarns worked just as well as the original
yarn since they have great structure and a wide array of colors in
the lineup.

A GOOD CHOICE

Yarn: 220 wool yarns from Cascade Yarns (100% wool;
100 g; 220 yds) in the following amounts and colors:

1 skein each of 220 Wool Heathers from Cascade Yarns:

A: 9455	**D:** 9324
B: 2422	**E:** 9449
C: 7811	**F:** 9453

1 skein each of 220 Wool from Cascade Yarns:

G: 8904	**I:** 8891
H: 8885	**J:** 9467

1 skein of 220 Wool Quatro from Cascade Yarns:

K: 9437

You can use any combination of these worsted-weight yarns;
when substituting yarns and colors, it's important to match
the values so the stripes are balanced visually.

Needles: Size 6 (4 mm) and size 8 (5 mm) needles, or size
needed to obtain guge

Knit in 220 Wool, 220 Wool Heathers, and
220 Wool Quatro from Cascade Yarns

Knit in Bangles
from Classic Elite Yarns

A NOT-SO-GOOD CHOICE

The nylon/viscose blend ribbon does
not work well for this project for two
reasons. First, it is too heavy to main-
tain the structural integrity of a large
garment such as this jacket. Second,
because it isn't a natural fiber yarn, it
has absolutely no memory. Like many
ribbons, it will tend to stretch out in
this larger jacket.

Ribbon does have great drape and this yarn would be wonderful knit in a
top-down design or in a garter stitch project that requires little shaping.

BULKY-WEIGHT YARN

These days, bulky-weight yarn is no longer banished to the craft section of big department stores. Bulky yarn can be comprised of any fiber and it is often the texture of the yarn rather than the fiber content that gives it bulk. Imagine bouncy bouclés and wide ribbons, plied combinations, and wrapped thick-and-thin yarns and you've got the picture.

Much of the yarn that we categorize as novelty yarn actually fits into the bulky category. Synthetic yarns can be fringed, wrapped with a binder, or plied with thinner strands of other fibers. Animal fibers can be brushed or looped (bouclé), and the way these fibers loft when knit can provide additional bulk.

FELTED ENTRELAC TOTE

CAPTIVATING CAPE

FAIR ISLE TOGGLE COAT

SELF-FRINGING AFGHAN

Knit in Baby Alpaca Grande from Plymouth Yarn Company

CAPTIVATING CAPE

By JoAnne Turcotte

For this garment, the amount of drape and stretch of the yarn are critical factors to consider. JoAnne chose Baby Alpaca Grande because it has incredible drape—perfect for a large circular cape. And, contrary to the notion that alpaca stretches terribly, this yarn does not necessarily stretch, making it the perfect fiber for a large, heavy cape.

This cape is knit from the top down in stockinette stitch. Evenly spaced increases make the cape grow larger in diameter every few rows. Knitting from the top down lets you adjust the final length as desired. The bottom trim and the button bands are worked in garter stitch to create an accent and to give the cape more weight at the bottom.

The Baby Alpaca Grande is a two-ply singles, which means it has two strands of loosely twisted yarn wrapped around each other. As a strand of yarn it has little elasticity or springiness. Knit up, the yarn does not stretch, which helps to keep this heavy garment at the correct length.

Skill level: Beginner ◖☐☐☐

Size: One size

Finished length: 22"

MATERIALS

Alpaca Grande from Plymouth Yarn Company (100% baby alpaca; 100 g; 110 yds)

 MC   8 skeins in color 2160

 CC   2 skeins in color 2020

Size 9 (5.5 mm) circular needle, 24" to 32" long

Size 10 (6 mm) circular needle, 24" to 32" long, or size needed to obtain gauge

Tapestry needle

3 buttons, 1¼" diameter

GAUGE

14 sts = 4" in St st on larger needle

CAPE

With smaller needle and MC, loosely CO 64 sts.

Row 1: K8, *(pm, K8); rep from * to end of row: 7 markers placed.

Knit 3 rows.

Change to larger needle and beg patt:

Row 1: *(K1f&b, knit to 1 st before marker, K1f&b); rep from * to end of row—16 sts total inc; 1 st at beg, 1 st on each side of marker, and 1 st at end.

Row 2: Purl.

Row 3: Knit.

Row 4: Purl.

Rows 5 and 6: Knit.

Work 6-row patt until piece measures 20" from beg, ending with row 6.

Change to CC and knit 10 rows, inc as before on first row only.

BO all sts loosely.

FINISHING

Buttonhole band: With MC, RS facing you and smaller needle, beg at right front edge, PU 77 sts along edge. Knit 1 row. Next row: Work 3 buttonholes evenly spaced along top 10" of edge by working each button-hole as (K2tog, YO). Knit 3 rows. BO all sts kw.

Button band: PU same number of sts along opposite front edge. Knit 5 rows. BO all sts kw.

Sew on 3 buttons across from buttonholes.

Weave in all ends. Block lightly if desired.

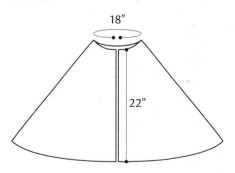

ALTERNATE **PICKS** AND **PANS**

Jungle is a wide ribbon that creates a lovely draping fabric. Ribbons are known to be slippery and stretchy and must be knit firmly. The slipperiness of ribbon also adds to its tendency to grow. A stockinette-stitch pattern is not firm enough to hold a slippery yarn in place. For a large cape such as this garment, the overall body of the cape needs to be knit firmly. To do so, JoAnne had to adjust the gauge to be tighter to help prevent stretching. Of course, knitting a tighter gauge also leads to less drape. Knitting the trim with a double strand of Furlauro added some weight to the bottom and more texture as well.

A GOOD CHOICE

Knit in Jungle with Furlauro trim, both from Plymouth Yarn Company

While the ribbon worked for this pattern, the true beauty of knitting with ribbon yarn is the incredible drape you can achieve. Using it for a more openwork pattern would showcase the yarn's beauty, but would create a much stretchier garment in the process.

Yarn:

> **MC** 15 balls of Jungle from Plymouth Yarn Company (100% nylon; 50 g; 61 yds) in color 744 copper
>
> **CC** 4 balls of Furlauro from Plymouth Yarn Company (100% nylon; 50 g; 82 yds) in color 744 copper

Needles: Size 9 (5.5 mm) and size 10 (6 mm) circular needles, each 24" to 32" long, or size needed to obtain gauge

Knit in Mauch Chunky from Kraemer Yarns

A NOT-SO-GOOD CHOICE

While we often think of wool as having memory and a degree of elasticity, this particular wool has no springiness because it is single ply and loosely spun. While it's a warm fiber with a great deal of bloom and fuzziness, it really didn't have any stretch or drape.

The Mauch Chunky worked up well at the given gauge, but the knit fabric didn't have enough weight to allow swing in the circular cape. If knit more firmly, the fabric might have more weight, which can help achieve drape, but it would not be fluid. This yarn would be a good choice for structured garments such as sweaters.

Knit in Lopi from Reynolds

FELTED ENTRELAC TOTE

By Donna Druchunas

Donna has a penchant for both felted bags and multicolored projects, but working with two or more colors at once can be challenging when it comes to felting. Color-work areas may shrink more than solid areas, and unfortunately knitters won't know this until a project is already knit and felted. To avoid this problem, Donna mixed stripes and entrelac, working large sections in each color. This also ensures that the colors remain distinct, because small color patterns may blur and blend together as the stitches shrink and become matted during the felting process.

Stockinette stitch works well for felting because it has no texture and in most cases any fancier stitch work would be lost in the felting process. Circular entrelac provides a fast way to combine colors in a project. The entrelac pattern is easy to memorize even though the instructions may seem daunting to a first-time entrelac knitter.

The 100%-wool Lopi is a "singles" (unplied) yarn. Because it's not plied, the fibers are free to move around during the felting process creating a smooth, dense felted fabric. The autumn colors create a sophisticated palette for this bag.

Skill level: Intermediate ■■■□

Size: Approx 16" x 22" after felting, excluding handles

Exact size is determined by felting.

MATERIALS

Lopi from Reynolds (100% Icelandic wool; 100 g; 110 yds)

A 2 skeins of color 9985 green

B 2 skeins of color 9964 gold

C 1 skein of color 9987 dark green

Size 15 (10 mm) circular needle, approx 24" long

Tapestry needle

2 D-shaped purse handles, 5" (12.5 cm) each

GAUGE

Approx 12 sts = 4" in St st before felting

Exact gauge is not critical. Make sure your stitches are light and airy to ensure fast and even felting.

PATTERN STITCHES

Stockinette Stitch (Circular)

Knit all rnds.

Stockinette Stitch (Back and Forth)

Row 1 (RS): Knit.

Row 2 (WS): Purl.

Rep rows 1 and 2 for patt.

TOTE

With A, CO 70 sts. Join to work in rnd, pm, being careful not to twist sts. Work stripe patt in St st as follows:

With A, knit 6 rnds.

With B, knit 2 rnds.

With A, knit 2 rnds.

With B, knit 2 rnds.

With A, knit 6 rnds.

Cut A.

Bottom Triangles

Row 1 (RS): With B, K2, turn.

Row 2: Purl 2, turn.

Row 3: Knit 3, turn.

Row 4: Purl 3, turn.

Row 5: Knit 4, turn.

Row 6: Purl 4, turn.

Row 7: Knit 5, turn.

Row 8: Purl 5, turn.

Row 9: Knit 6, turn.

Row 10: Purl 6, turn.

Row 11: Knit 7, turn.

Do not turn. Rep rows 1–11 until 10 triangles are complete. Cut B.

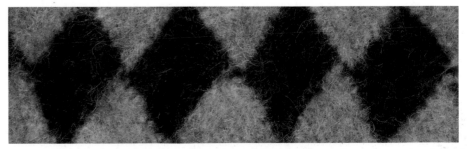

Large sections of each color are worked in the entrelac pattern.

First Set of Rectangles (Right Slanting)

*With WS facing you and A, PU and purl 7 sts along side of triangle.

Row 1 (RS): K7.

Row 2 (WS): P6, P2tog.

Rep rows 1 and 2 until there are no more sts to join.

Rep from * until 10 rectangles are complete. Cut A.

Second Set of Rectangles (Left Slanting)

*With RS facing you and B, PU and knit 7 sts along side of triangle.

Row 1 (WS): P7.

Row 2 (RS): K6, ssk.

Rep rows 1 and 2 until there are no more sts to join.

Rep from * until 10 rectangles are complete. Cut B.

Third Set of Rectangles (Right Slanting)

With C, rep first set of rectangles.

Fourth Set of Rectangles (Left Slanting)

With B, rep second set of rectangles.

Fifth Set of Rectangles (Right Slanting)

With A, rep first set of rectangles.

Top Triangles

With RS facing you and B, PU 7 sts along edge of rectangle.

Row 1: Purl 7.

Row 2: K6, ssk.

Row 3: Purl 6.

Row 4: K5, ssk.

Row 5: Purl 5.

Row 6: K4, ssk.

Row 7: Purl 4.

Row 8: K3, ssk.

Row 9: Purl 3.

Row 10: K2, ssk.

Row 11: Purl 2.

Row 12: K1, ssk.

Row 13: Purl 1.

Row 14: Ssk.

Rep rows 1–14 until 10 triangles have been completed—70 sts.

Cut B.

With A, knit 6 rnds.

HANDLE FLAPS

K35, turn, leaving rem 35 sts unworked.

*Working back and forth on these 35 sts, work 5 more rows in St st.

Dec row (RS): Ssk, knit to last 2 sts, K2tog.

Next row: Purl.

Rep last 2 rows until 25 sts rem.

Change to C and work 12 rows in St st.

BO all sts.

Rep from * on rem 35 sts.

Sew bottom seam closed. Weave in ends.

FELTING

Put bag and strap in a zippered pillowcase to catch lint, and toss into the washing machine with an old towel or blue jeans. Set machine for smallest load size with a hot wash and cold rinse, and add a very small amount of soap. Check felting every few minutes. Some yarns will felt within the first few minutes, while others may take two or three cycles. When fibers are matted and you don't want the bag to shrink any more, take it out and gently rinse in the sink. Roll bag in a towel and squeeze out excess water.

FINISHING

If necessary, stretch bag into shape and then dry flat. When bag is thoroughly dry, fold flaps to the outside over handles and sew in place. Bury ends inside flap and knot in place if desired.

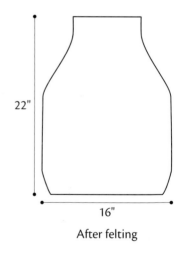

22"

16"

After felting

ALTERNATE **PICKS** AND **PANS**

For this bag, Donna used a wool/mohair blend yarn that also felted wonderfully.

A GOOD CHOICE

Sometimes mohair-blend yarn is fuzzier than a pure-wool yarn, but that wasn't true in this case. The bright colors make for a fun and funky result that is completely different in style than the subtle autumn colors in the first bag. If your bag comes out very fuzzy and you prefer a smoother texture, any stray fibers can be sheared off with sharp sewing scissors.

Yarn: Lamb's Pride Bulky from Brown Sheep Company (85% wool, 15% mohair; 4 oz/113 g; 125 yds/114 m)

  A   2 skeins of color M-110 Orange You Glad

  B   2 skeins of color M-56 Clematis

  C   1 skein of color M-120 Limeade

Needles: Size 15 (10 mm) circular needle, 24" long, or size needed to obtain gauge

Knit in Lamb's Pride Bulky
from Brown Sheep Company

A NOT-SO-GOOD CHOICE

Knit in Lamb's Pride
Superwash Worsted
from Brown Sheep Company

While Lamb's Pride Superwash is by the same company as the previous example, superwash wool yarn is treated so it can be machine washed. This feature makes it great for sweaters, socks, and other wearables, but it's not suitable for felting.

Make sure you always choose 100% wool or a yarn with a high wool content blended with mohair, llama, or alpaca for felting. A very small percentage of man-made fiber may be included in a felting project, but if you want to try something like this, be sure to knit and felt a swatch before investing the time and money into making a large project only to discover that it will not shrink when you try to felt it.

Knit in 128 Tweed from Cascade Yarns

FAIR ISLE TOGGLE COAT

By Celeste Pinheiro

Knit coats are very luxurious and cozy, but need special consideration when it comes to choosing a yarn. They really need a hard-wearing, sturdy yarn, and require a pattern that has the structural support of seams and a firm button band so that the coat will hang straight and not stretch out of shape. Using a plied fiber that is light and strong with a good twist, such as basic wool like the Cascade 128 Tweed used here, will enable the fabric to wear well and stand up to the rougher exposure a coat gets.

When embarking on a large multicolored project such as this Fair Isle coat that involves a lot of time, effort, and stranding, it's best to work with contrasting colors of a yarn that's not fuzzy, fussy, or complicated.

Skill level: Experienced ◀■■■▶

Sizes: Women's S (M, L, XL, 2X)

Finished bust: 36 (40, 44, 48, 52)"

Finished length: 34 (35, 35, 36, 36)"

MATERIALS

128 Tweed from Cascade Yarns (90% Peruvian highland wool, 10% Donegal; 100 g; 128 yds)

MC	8 (9, 10, 11, 12) skeins of color 7616
A	2 skeins of color 7617
B	2 skeins of color 7626
C	2 skeins of color 7615
D	2 skeins of color 7627

Size 9 (5.5 mm) needles

Size 10½ (6.5 mm) needles, or size needed to obtain gauge

Tapestry needle

5 (5, 5, 6, 6) toggle buttons, approx 2" long

GAUGE

14 sts and 18 rows = 4" in Fair Isle patt using larger needles

The cast-on numbers include 1 st at each side for selvage. Work the Fair Isle chart and any shaping between these selvage stitches. Work the beginning selvage stitch in the same color as the first stitch of the row and the ending selvage stitch in the same color as the last stitch of the row.

The Fair Isle motifs show up nicely when the main color is supported by four secondary colors that contrast without distracting.

FAIR ISLE BEGINNING-STITCH CHART

Work 1 edge st and then beg chart on indicated st for your size.

SIZES	BACK beg st	LEFT FRONT beg st	RIGHT FRONT beg st	SLEEVES beg st
S	6	6	4	6
M	5	5	4	6
L	5	5	4	5
1X	1	1	4	5
2X	1	1	4	5

BACK

With smaller needles and MC, CO 65 (73, 79, 87, 93) sts.

Knit 7 rows, ending with WS row.

Note that the Fair Isle chart (on page 84) is an odd number of rows. On the first rep, row 1 is a RS row. When you beg the second rep, row 1 will be a WS row.

Next row (RS): Change to larger needles, working in St st and keeping 1 st at each side as selvage st, work all rows of Fair Isle chart beg on st indicated for your size in table above, purl on RS rows 5 and 21. Rep all rows of Fair Isle chart, then rep rows 1 and 2; ending with RS row.

Next row: Change to smaller needles and MC, purl 3 rows.

Next row: Change to larger needles, work ribbing chart until piece measures 26 (26½, 26, 26½, 26½)" from beg, ending with WS row.

Armhole shaping: BO 4 sts at beg of next 2 rows, BO 2 sts at beg of next 2 rows, then dec 1 st at each side EOR 4 times (working K2tog on RS, and ssk on WS)—45 (53, 59, 67, 73) sts.

Keeping in est patt, work even until piece measures 34 (35, 35, 36, 36)" from beg.

BO all sts.

LEFT FRONT

With smaller needles and MC, CO 31 (35, 38, 42, 45). Work as for back (beg on st indicated for your size in table above) until piece measures 26 (26½, 26, 26½, 26½)" from beg, ending with WS row.

Armhole shaping: Cont in est patt, BO at armhole edge on EOR 4 sts once, 2 sts once, and then 1 st 4 times—21 (25, 28, 32, 35) sts.

Work even in est patt until piece measures 32 (32½, 32½, 33, 33)" from beg, ending with RS row.

Neck shaping: Cont in est patt, BO at neck edge on EOR 6 (4, 4, 4, 5) sts once, 4 sts 0 (0, 0, 1, 1) times, 3 sts 1 (2, 2, 1, 1) once, 2 sts once, and 1 st once—9 (12, 15, 18, 20) sts in shoulder.

Work even in est patt until piece measures 34 (35, 35, 36, 36)" from beg.

BO all sts.

Right Front

With smaller needles and MC, CO 31 (35, 38, 42, 45). Work as for back beg on st indicated for your size in table above) until piece measures 26 (26½, 26, 26½, 26½)" from beg, ending with RS row.

Armhole shaping: Cont in est patt, BO at armhole edge on EOR 4 sts once, 2 sts once, and then 1 st 4 times—21 (25, 28, 32, 35) sts.

Work even in est patt until piece measures 32 (32½, 32½, 33, 33)" from beg, ending with WS row.

Neck shaping: Cont in est patt, BO at neck edge on EOR 6 (4, 4, 4, 5) sts once, 4 sts 0 (0, 0, 1, 1) times, 3 sts 1 (2, 2, 1, 1) once, 2 sts once, and 1 st once—9 (12, 15, 18, 20) sts in shoulder.

Work even in est patt until piece measures 34 (35, 35, 36, 36)" from beg.

BO all sts.

SLEEVES

With smaller needles and MC, CO 41 (41, 43, 43, 43) sts.

Knit 7 rows, ending with WS row.

Change to larger needle, work Fair Isle chart (beg on st indicated for your size in table above) through row 2 of second rep, ending on RS row.

Change to smaller needles and MC, purl 3 rows.

Change to larger needles, cont in rib patt, AT SAME TIME inc 1 st at each side every 8 (8, 8, 6, 6) rows

3 (5, 6, 8, 9) times—47 (51, 55, 59, 61) sts.

Sleeve cap: BO 4 sts at beg of next 2 rows—39 (43, 47, 51, 53) sts. Keeping in rib patt, dec 1 st at each side EOR 14 (16, 18, 20, 21) times—11 sts rem, BO all sts

FINISHING

Sew shoulder seams, sew in sleeves. Sew underarm and side seams, making sure side seams measure 26 (26½, 26, 26½, 26½)" from beg.

Front edges: With RS facing you, smaller needles, and MC, PU 116 (119, 119, 123, 123) sts along left front edge and knit 5 rows. BO all sts. Rep for right front edge.

Collar: With WS facing you, larger needles and MC, PU 81 (87, 87, 93, 93) sts along neckline; this includes 1 st at each side for selvage, plus 1 more st to balance the patt. After the last rep of the 6-st patt, work the first st of the patt rep one more time before the ending selvage st. On next RS row, beg Fair Isle chart starting on row 17, work through row 23, work rows 1–16, and then rows 1 and 2, ending with WS row. Change to MC, knit 6 rows, BO all sts loosely.

Facing: With RS facing you and smaller needle, attach MC and PU 27 sts along the Fair Isle portion of the short edge of the collar; do not pick up along the garter st rows. Work 5 rows in St st. BO all sts. Sew facing to WS of collar. Rep on other end of collar.

Loops and toggles: From MC, cut 30 (30, 36, 36, 36) pieces of yarn, each 12" long. Using 3 groups of 2 strands each, braid the strands. Fold braid in half and attach folded end to right band approx 5 (5, 6, 6, 6)" apart. Sew toggle button opposite loop, and knot ends of braided loop to fit around toggle snuggly. Make 5 (5, 6, 6, 6) loops.

Fair Isle chart
(worked in St st)

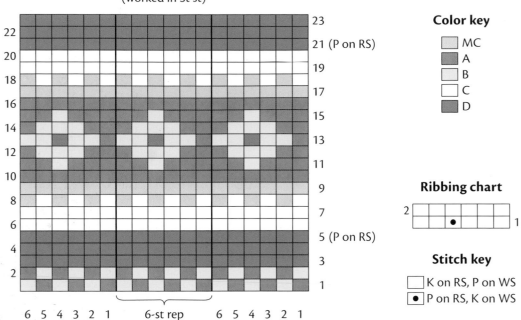

6 5 4 3 2 1 | 6-st rep | 6 5 4 3 2 1

Color key

▢	MC
▨	A
▨	B
▢	C
▨	D

Ribbing chart

2 [▢ ▢ • ▢ ▢] 1

Stitch key

▢ K on RS, P on WS
• P on RS, K on WS

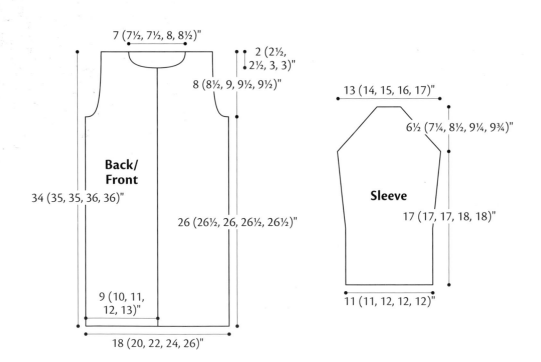

7 (7½, 7½, 8, 8½)"

2 (2½, 2½, 3, 3)"

8 (8½, 9, 9½, 9½)"

Back/Front

34 (35, 35, 36, 36)"

26 (26½, 26, 26½, 26½)"

9 (10, 11, 12, 13)"

18 (20, 22, 24, 26)"

13 (14, 15, 16, 17)"

6½ (7¼, 8½, 9¼, 9¾)"

Sleeve

17 (17, 17, 18, 18)"

11 (11, 12, 12, 12)"

ALTERNATE **PICKS** AND **PANS**

Duchess, a merino/cashmere blend, shows the stitches well, and seems to

A GOOD CHOICE

support itself nicely in the final coat. It also exhibits strong wear-ability because of its firm twist and several plies. This yarn is a bit heavier and denser than the 128 Tweed used in the original garment. The weight of the finished coat could cause it to stretch out of shape, but the firm twist of the multiple-ply yarn should help it retain its shape.

Yarn: Duchess from Classic Elite Yarns (40% merino, 28% viscose, 10% cashmere, 15% nylon, 7% angora; 50 g; 75 yds) in the following amounts and colors:

MC 14 (15, 16, 17, 18) skeins of 1095

A 2 (2, 3, 3, 3) skeins of 1077

B 2 (2, 2, 3, 3) skeins of 1068

C 2 (2, 2, 3, 3) skeins of 1085

D 2 (2, 2, 3, 3) skeins of 1025

Needles: Size 9 (5.5 mm) and size 10½ (6.5 mm) needles or size needed to obtain gauge

A NOT-SO-GOOD CHOICE

Knit in Baby Alpaca Grande
by Plymouth Yarn Company

Baby Alpaca Grande yarn is more loosely spun, and is heavier than the wool tweed. While this yarn worked well for the cape on page 73, it could pose a problem in this design. Although this alpaca has less stretch than most, alpaca is not as springy as wool, and therefore does not have as much memory. It may stretch out in the rib portion of the coat, most likely in length, but probably also in width, because sitting while wearing a garment such as this puts a lot of stretch stress on it. Also, the looser-spun alpaca will not wear well as a coat—a garment that tends to be rubbed and bumped up against rough surfaces.

Knit in Duchess from Classic Elite Yarns

Knit in Adelph from Cherry Tree Hill Yarn

SELF-FRINGING AFGHAN

By Cheryl Potter

The bold colors of the solid yarn combined with the bouclé allow for clear pattern definition on this striped afghan. The solid color is wrapped with a binder filled with bits of color, which adds interest without distracting from the garter-stitch pattern. Although this yarn is considered bulky, it knit up as a light bulky, and the bouclé was very bouncy and the fabric draped beautifully. Both sides can be considered the "right side" on the afghan. The superwash yarn makes this afghan practical as well as beautiful—and it's a natural-fiber project.

This beginner afghan requires no finishing work. It can be as large or small as you desire (or that the yarn will allow). Stitches for this afghan were cast on for the length and worked until the desired width. Although it can be difficult to find long enough needles, you can also work with two circular needles, 29" long.

Whether knitting this afghan vertically or horizontally, the beauty of this afghan is that you can stop once the desired width or length is achieved. The last row knit is the end of the afghan; no finishing work is required because you fringe as you go.

Skill level: Beginner ◼☐☐◻

Size: Approx 60" wide x 80" long. The stripes can run lengthwise (CO 250 sts) or crosswise (CO 180 sts).

MATERIALS

Adelph from Cherry Tree Hill Yarn (92% washable wool, 8% textured nepp binder; 50 g; 78 yds) in the following colorways

A	7 balls of Rust
B	7 balls of Teal
C	7 balls of Plum
D	7 balls of Raspberry
E	7 balls of Gold

Size 10 (6 mm) circular needle, 60" long, *or* 2 circular needles, 29" long (put a point protector on one end of each so that stitches will not slip off as you are knitting)

GAUGE

12 sts = 4" in garter st

AFGHAN

With A, leaving a tail of 7", CO 250 sts (for lengthwise stripes or 180 sts for crosswise stripes), break yarn, leaving a 7" tail.

Rows 1–4: With A, leaving a 7" tail, knit to end and break yarn, leaving a 7 " tail.

Cont in 4-row garter st with each of the rem colors: B, then C, then D, then E. As you complete each color, take all tails from that color and tie them in firm overhand knot (see below) at each end of knitting. Rep color sequence until afghan is desired length, ending with 4 rows of E. Wait to trim ends until afghan is complete.

Trim ends and block lightly.

Overhand knot

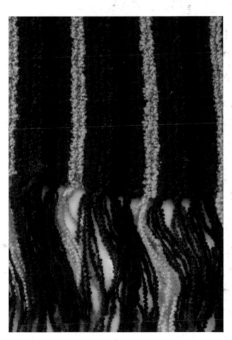

This afghan can be knit horizontally or vertically with equal success.

ALTERNATE **PICKS** AND **PANS**

For this version, a slightly thicker hand-painted Merino bouclé was used in five colorways. Stitches for this version were cast on for the width first, which made the project easier to handle, and then worked until the desired length. The result is the same sized afghan as the previous example, only in a different direction. This horizontally knit afghan will retain its shape better than the one that was knit vertically because of the tendency for vertical knitting to stretch.

A GOOD CHOICE

The colorways were sequenced to pull colors from each successive colorway and this was a lot of fun to coordinate. Because the colorways were run horizontally, the colors in the hand-painted yarn created wider stripes, resulting in a subtle watercolor effect without pooling or striping.

Knit in Merino Boucle from Cherry Tree Hill Yarn

The texture and the color changes were a lot to handle and the afghan was a little busy. It may have been better to use a less textural yarn since so many different colorways were incorporated. If you want to use such a highly textured yarn, try alternating only two or three colorways instead. Also this yarn is not superwash; the afghan would have to be hand washed or dry-cleaned.

Yarn: Merino Bouclé from Cherry Tree Hill Yarn (100% merino wool; 8 oz; 365 yds):

A	1 hank of Moody Blues	**D**	1 hank of Winterberry	
B	1 hank of Champlain Sunset	**E**	1 hank of Tropical Storm	
C	1 hank of Dusk			

Needles: Size 10 (6 mm) circular needle, 60" long, or 2 circular needles, 29" long, or size needed to obtain gauge

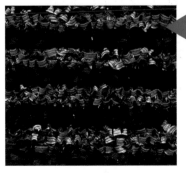

A NOT-SO-GOOD CHOICE

This swatch was knit from novelty yarns and synthetic fibers, specifically a series of wide ribbons. The ribbons were slippery and difficult to work with. They tended to stretch and to create open spaces between each stitch and each yarn that would only get larger with time. Even though only two colorways were used to minimize the busy look, the overall effect was distracting. The yarn easily snagged on other items and was not very practical.

*Knit in Calypso
from South West Trading
Company*

By nature an afghan needs to be warm and comforting. This yarn does not have such characteristics. Delicate ribbon with glitter and fringe is not suited to a large, somewhat heavy project that will get a lot of use, and requires durability. Because this ribbon has so much texture and color, it needs a simple draped design such as a shawl or poncho, to show the fabric to its best advantage. With this fancy novelty yarn, a little goes a long way, making it great for fringe, trim, and embellishment.

ABBREVIATIONS AND GLOSSARY

Use the following to familiarize yourself with new terms or check abbreviations for stitches and techniques you may already know.

approx	approximately
beg	begin(ning)
BO	bind off
CC	contrasting color
cn	cable needle(s)
CO	cast on
cont	continue(ing)(s)
dec(s)	decrease(ing)(s)
dpn(s)	double-pointed needle(s)
EOR	every other row
est	establish(ed)
g	gram(s)
garter st	garter stitch [back and forth: knit every row; in the round: knit 1 round, purl 1 round]
inc(s)	increase(ing)(s)
K	knit
K1f&b	knit into front and back of same stitch—1 stitch increased
K2tog	knit 2 stitches together—1 stitch decreased
K3tog	knit 3 stitches together—2 stitches decreased
kw	knitwise
LH	left hand
m	meter(s)
MC	main color
mm	millimeter(s)
oz	ounce(s)
P	purl
P2tog	purl 2 stitches together—1 stitch decreased
P3tog	purl 3 stitches together—2 stitches decreased
patt(s)	pattern(s)
pm	place marker
psso	pass slipped stitch over
PU	pick up and knit
pw	purlwise
rem	remain(ing)
rep(s)	repeat(s)
rev	reverse
rev sc	reverse single crochet
RH	right hand
rnd(s)	round(s)
RS	right side
sc	single crochet
sl	slip
sl st	slip stitch purlwise unless otherwise instructed
sl 1 kw-K1-psso	slip 1 knitwise, knit 1, pass slipped stitch over—1 stitch decreased
sl 1 kw-K2tog-psso	slip 1 knitwise, knit 2 stitches together, pass slipped stitch over—2 stitches decreased
ssk	slip, slip, knit [slip 2 stitches knitwise, one at a time, to right needle, then insert left needle from left to right into front loops and knit 2 stitches together—1 stitch decreased]
st(s)	stitch(es)
St st	stockinette stitch [knit on right side, purl on wrong side]
tbl	through back loop(s)
tog	together
WS	wrong side
wyib	with yarn in back
wyif	with yarn in front
yd(s)	yard(s)
YO	yarn over

TECHNIQUES

In this section you'll find a compilation of special techniques. The descriptions are by no means exhaustive, but you may find them handy for quick reference.

CABLE CAST ON

To cast on stitches to a work that's already in progress, such as to add sleeve stitches to a shirt, the cable-cast-on method is a quick and easy option.

At the beginning of a row of knitting, insert the right needle between the first two stitches on the left needle, wrap the yarn around the needle as if to knit, and pull the new loop through to the front and place it on the end of the left needle to form one new stitch. Repeat for the number of stitches required.

Insert needle between
two stitches. Knit a stitch.

Place new stitch
on left needle.

PROVISIONAL CAST ON

A provisional cast on is temporary, and will be removed later so that the live stitches remain intact.

1. Use a crochet hook and make a number of loose chain stitches with a contrasting slippery yarn, such as a mercerized cotton. Make one chain for each stitch that will be cast on the needle plus a few extra.

2. Using a knitting needle, knit into the back of each chain with the yarn that will be used in the pattern. Begin knitting as instructed in the pattern.

3. To pick up the stitches, remove the crochet chain by pulling each chain out one at a time and placing the live stitches back on the knitting needle.

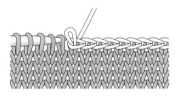

CROCHET

Crochet is often used in conjunction with knitting for finishing edges, making embellishments, adding buttonholes, and joining seams.

Chain Stitch

To begin, make a slipknot. Place the yarn over the hook and draw through the loop on the hook to start the chain. Repeat for desired number of chain stitches.

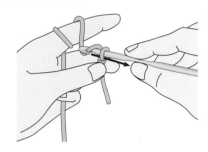

Single Crochet

Single crochet is often used to finish a knit edge. To work single crochet, begin with a chain stitch. Insert the hook into the first stitch, *wrap the yarn over the hook and draw it through the stitch (two loops on the hook), and then wrap the yarn over the hook again and draw through both loops on the hook; one stitch is made. Insert the hook into the next stitch and repeat from * to end.

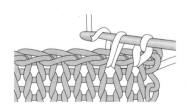

Reverse Single Crochet

Reverse single crochet (also known as crab stitch) gives the stitches a twisted appearance. The edge will be slightly raised, making a nice decorative finish for bound-off or cast-on edges.

To work reverse single crochet, with the right side of the project facing you, insert the hook into the first stitch below the cast-on or bound-off edge, starting at the left end of your work. Wrap the yarn over the hook, pull the loop through the knitting, wrap the yarn over the hook again, and pull through both loops on the hook; one stitch is made. Repeat, working from left to right to the end of the row or round.

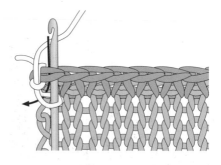

INCREASES

Increases are used to shape various parts of a knit project, such as armholes or necklines on a sweater. The following types of increases are used in this book.

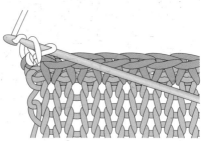

Make One

Insert the right needle under the bar of yarn between the last stitch knit and the next stitch to be knit. Lift the bar onto the left needle and knit into the back of the stitch. One stitch made.

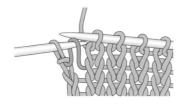

Insert left needle from front to back through "running thread."

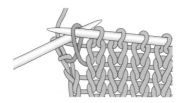

Knit into back of stitch.

Knit in Front and Back of Stitch

Insert the right needle into the designated stitch on the left needle where the increase is to be made. Knit as usual, but do not slip the original stitch off of the left needle. Move the right needle behind the left needle and knit into the back of the same stitch. Slip the original stitch off the left needle.

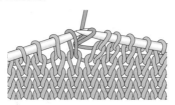

Knit into stitch but do not drop it off left needle.

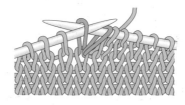

Knit into back of same stitch.

THREE-NEEDLE BIND OFF

The three-needle bind off is used to join shoulder seams in one step, rather than binding off both the front and back stitches and then sewing them together. The result is a less bulky seam.

Place the knit pieces right sides together with the needles parallel and pointing in the same direction. Knit one stitch from the front needle and one stitch from the back needle together. Repeat, and then pass the first knit stitch over the second stitch to bind off one stitch. Continue in the same manner until all stitches have been bound off.

Knit together 1 stitch from front needle and 1 stitch from back.

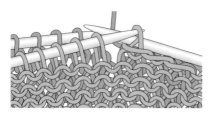

Bind off.

KITCHENER STITCH

Thread the yarn tail onto a tapestry needle. Place the knit pieces wrong sides together with needles parallel; you will now have a front needle and a back needle. Work with the tapestry needle and always keep the yarn beneath the needle as you work.

1. Insert the tapestry needle into the first stitch on the front needle as if to knit, pull the yarn through and take the stitch off the needle.

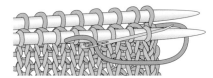

2. Insert the tapestry needle into the next stitch on the front needle as if to purl, pull the thread through and leave the stitch on the needle.

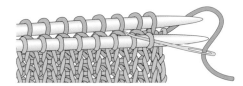

3. Insert the tapestry into the first stitch on the back needle as if to purl, pull the yarn through and take the stitch off the needle.

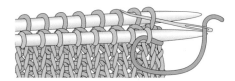

4. Insert the tapestry needle into the next stitch on the back needle as if to knit, pull the yarn through and leave the stitch on the needle.

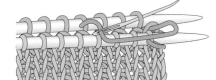

5. Insert the tapestry needle into the stitch that was left on the front needle as if to knit, pull the yarn through and take the stitch off the needle.

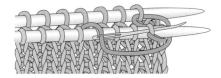

Repeat steps 2–5 until all stitches are removed.

USEFUL INFORMATION

STANDARD YARN-WEIGHT SYSTEM

Yarn-Weight Categories and Symbols	0 Lace	1 Super Fine	2 Fine	3 Light	4 Medium	5 Bulky	6 Super Bulky
Types of Yarn in Category	Fingering 10-count crochet thread	Sock, Fingering, Baby	Sport, Baby	DK, Light Worsted	Worsted, Afghan, Aran	Chunky, Craft, Rug	Bulky, Roving
Knit Gauge Ranges in Stockinette Stitch to 4"	33 to 40** sts	27 to 32 sts	23 to 26 sts	21 to 24 sts	16 to 20 sts	12 to 15 sts	6 to 11 sts
Recommended Needle in Metric Size Range	1.5 to 2.25 mm	2.25 to 3.25 mm	3.25 to 3.75 mm	3.75 to 4.5 mm	4.5 to 5.5 mm	5.5 to 8 mm	8 mm and larger
Recommended Needle in U.S. Size Range	000 to 1	1 to 3	3 to 5	5 to 7	7 to 9	9 to 11	11 and larger

SKILL LEVELS

■☐☐☐ **Beginner:** Projects for first-time knitters using basic knit and purl stitches. Minimal shaping.

■■☐☐ **Easy:** Projects using basic stitches, repetitive stitch patterns, simple color changes, and simple shaping and finishing.

■■■☐ **Intermediate:** Projects with a variety of stitches, such as basic cables and lace, simple intarsia, double-pointed needles and knitting-in-the-round techniques, and mid-level shaping and finishing.

■■■■ **Experienced:** Projects using advanced techniques and stitches, such as short rows, fair isle, more intricate intarsia, cables, lace patterns, and numerous color changes.

METRIC CONVERSION

Use these handy formulas to easily convert yards to meters, or vice versa, so you can calculate how much yarn you'll need for your project.

Yards x .914 = meters

Meters x 1.093 = yards

Grams x .035 = ounces

Ounces x 28.35 = grams

RESOURCES

Check your local yarn shop, or visit the Web sites below to find the yarns used in this book.

ADRIAFIL
www.adriafil.com
Carezza

BRISTOL YARN GALLERY
www.plymouthyarn.com
Buckingham
Lyndon Hill

BROWN SHEEP COMPANY, INC.
www.brownsheep.com
Cotton Fleece
Lamb's Pride Bulky
Lamb's Pride Worsted

CASCADE YARNS, INC.
www.cascadeyarns.com
128 Tweed
220 Wool
220 Wool Heathers
220 Wool Quatro
Fun
Inca Alpaca
Sassy Stripes

CHERRY TREE HILL YARN
www.cherryyarn.com
Adelph
Cascade Fingering
Glitter Alpaca
Merino Boucle
North Country Cotton
Possum Worsted
Potluck Worsted
Silk and Merino DK
Soft Angora
Supersock

CLASSIC ELITE YARNS
www.classiceliteyarns.com
Bangles
Duchess
La Gran Mohair
Minnie

FROG TREE YARNS
www.frogtreeyarns.com
Fingering-Weight Alpaca

LANE CERVINIA
(Various Web sites carry Lane
Cervina yarns)
Super Taj Mahal

JAMIESON AND SMITH
(Various Web sites carry Jamieson
and Smith yarns)
Shetland Jumper-Weight Wool

KRAEMER YARNS
www.kraemeryarnshop.com
Mauch Chunky

MISSION FALLS
www.missionfalls.com
1824 Cotton

MOUNTAIN COLORS
www.mountaincolors.com
Bearfoot

PLYMOUTH YARN COMPANY
www.plymouthyarn.com
Baby Alpaca Grande
Boku
*Buckingham from Bristol Yarn
Gallery (distributed by Plymouth
Yarn)*
Encore Colorspun Worsted
Furlauro
Jungle
Linen Isle
*Lyndon Hill from Bristol Yarn Gallery
(distributed by Plymouth Yarn)*
*Super Taj Mahal from Lane Cervinia
(distributed by Plymouth Yarn)*

REYNOLDS/JCA
(Various Web sites carry Reynolds/
JCA yarns)
Lopi
Soft Sea Wool

ROWAN CLASSIC YARNS
www.ryclassic.com
Cashsoft Baby DK

SCHOOLHOUSE PRESS
www.schoolhousepress.com

SOUTH WEST TRADING COMPANY
www.soysilk.com
Bamboo
Calypso

S. R. KERTZER
www.kertzer.com
Butterfly Cotton

WINDY VALLEY MUSKOX
www.windyvalleymuskox.com
Qiviut

KNITTING AND CROCHET TITLES

KNITTING

200 Knitted Blocks

365 Knitting Stitches a Year: Perpetual Calendar

A to Z of Knitting

Fair Isle Sweaters Simplified

First Knits

Fun and Funky Knitting

Funky Chunky Knitted Accessories

Handknit Skirts

Handknit Style II

Kitty Knits—*New!*

Knit One, Stripe Too

The Knitter's Book of Finishing Techniques

Knitting Beyond the Basics

Knitting Circles around Socks

Knitting with Gigi

The Little Box of Knits for Baby

The Little Box of Knitted Gifts

The Little Box of Knitted Throws

The Little Box of Socks—*New!*

Modern Classics

More Sensational Knitted Socks

Ocean Breezes

Pursenalities

Pursenality Plus

Romantic Style

Sensational Knitted Socks

Silk Knits

Simple Gifts for Dog Lovers—*New!*

Special Little Knits from Just One Skein

Stitch Style: Mittens

Stitch Style: Socks

Stripes, Stripes, Stripes—*New!*

Too Cute!

Top Down Sweaters

Wrapped in Comfort

The Yarn Stash Workbook

CROCHET

365 Crochet Stitches a Year: Perpetual Calendar

Amigurumi World—*New!*

A to Z of Crochet—*New!*

Crochet for Tots

Crocheted Pursenalities

Crocheted Socks!

First Crochet

Fun and Funky Crochet

The Little Box of Crochet for Baby

The Little Box of Crocheted Gifts

The Little Box of Crocheted Scarves

The Little Box of Crocheted Throws

Martingale®
& C O M P A N Y

America's Best-Loved Craft & Hobby Books®
America's Best-Loved Knitting Books®

Our books are available at bookstores and your favorite craft, fabric, and yarn retailers.
If you don't see the title you're looking for, visit us at **www.martingale-pub.com** or contact us at:

1-800-426-3126

International: 1-425-483-3313
Fax: 1-425-486-7596 • Email: info@martingale-pub.com

1/08 Knit